MISSION POSSIBLE

MISSION POSSIBLE

How to Achieve All Your Family Foundation's Goals

ISBN 978-1-5445-0520-6 Paperback

978-1-5445-0519-0 Ebook

BRUCE RAABE

MISSION POSSIBLE

HOW TO ACHIEVE ALL YOUR FAMILY FOUNDATION'S GOALS

CONTENTS

With Gratitude

To Dale Matheny, for his mentorship.

To Ruth Collins, for her knowledge and advice.

To my clients, who have taught me the importance and meaning of philanthropy.

To John Bowen, who has inspired me to finally tackle this project.

I do get some pleasure out of this ability to give, particularly to something where people are really slogging at it in the face of great adversity, to do some good in the world.

—Stanley Smith, May & Stanley Smith Charitable Trust

INTRODUCTION

I AM A PROBLEM SOLVER.

I have spent more than twenty-five years working closely with family foundations as their Chief Investment Officer, or CIO. I love helping families solve some of the complex challenges they face when managing their family foundation's assets. I especially love helping to make a reality these families' deep desire to give back and live lives rooted in generosity.

The problems I help solve facilitate the type of funding that effects big, important change, impacting deserving people and organizations in very real ways. As a result, the family members behind the family foundations I serve have the opportunity and freedom to focus on what's most important to them—collaborating to improve the areas of life they care most about.

Family foundations are set apart from other philanthropic endeavors because, in addition to charitable objectives, most family foundations also have the personal goal of working *together* to make a difference in their community. In the past twenty-five years, I have learned that, aside from managing investments and laying the groundwork for objectives to be achieved, what often helps foundations the most is the calming influence of a seasoned, independent third party. I make it my mission to ensure that the process of getting a family to their stated goals is fulfilling and collaborative.

As a professional CIO, I am compensated for my work with family foundations. Financial awards aside, however, I consider it a privilege to add the value of my own experience and expertise to foundations that are making an active effort to solve real problems in our society, whether on a local or global level. Beyond simply imagining this better future, these families are actively participating in *creating* that future. I am proud to be a part of that process.

What Is a Family Foundation?

There are many types of foundations, but family foundations are particularly compelling. Throughout this book, I will often use the word "foundation" as shorthand to refer to family foundations.

Family foundations are legally a subset of private foundations, which include family, corporate, independent, and operating foundations. Not only do foundations allow families to leave a legacy specific to their passion, personal history, community, and life's work, but they also provide the opportunity for family members to come together to give back collectively and collaboratively.

This is the idea, at least. The practice of actually running a family foundation can often look a little different.

> In this day and age of never-before-seen transparency, intense scrutiny, and digital media, innocent errors and mistakes can lead to collateral and reputational damage.

Many foundations fail to account for the specific rules and regulations that dictate what they can and cannot do in terms of structure, investment, and giving. In this day and age of never-before-seen transparency, intense scrutiny, and digital media, innocent errors and mistakes can lead to collateral and reputational damage. On a more human level, foundations also often don't think through the very real issue of family dynamics and how they come into play in a foundation setting.

According to the Council on Foundations, today there are over forty thousand family foundations with combined assets in excess of $300 billion, making grants of approximately *$20 billion per year* in support of organizations and causes that are meaningful to them. This trend in giving has grown generation over generation, and the amount of money in family foundations today is unprecedented. Many of the families behind these acts of generosity are largely unheralded for the work they do and change they effect.

Despite common perception, it's not just billionaires who start foundations. Families of varied income levels are putting their hard-earned money toward supporting those organizations, communities, and causes that they believe in the most. They are, quite literally, changing the world in ways both large and small, globally and locally.

In many ways, this phenomenon is uniquely American, and something we should all be proud of. A recent report by the Charities Aid Foundation found that America is the world's most generous nation, and that its citizens give the most to charity. We are fortunate to live in a society that offers entrepreneurs unparalleled opportunity. Combined with a culture that breeds generosity in a way not many places in the world do, there is a great potential to effect major change on many fronts.

My Personal Story

Everything changed for me at 5:04 p.m. on October 17, 1989. Up to this moment, I was a civil engineer living in Davis, California, working for CalTrans, the state's Department of Transportation. My job was to design and build bridges for California's vast highway network. It was an exciting career—applying state-of-the-art design tools while working with diverse teams to upgrade and expand our state's infrastructure.

But at that exact moment, the devastating 6.9-magnitude Loma Prieta earthquake shook the Bay Area—and my career.

Because the San Francisco Giants and Oakland A's were about to begin Game 3 of the World Series, the typically packed freeways were virtually empty. This was a true miracle, because major portions of the Bay Area freeway network were damaged or destroyed. The double-decker Cypress freeway in Oakland collapsed on itself, resulting in the majority of the sixty-three fatalities that day.

I was immediately dispatched to San Francisco to shore up the damaged Embarcadero Freeway. This double-decked concrete bridge, spanning over a mile of the San Francisco waterfront, matched the design of the Cypress but somehow remained standing.

I spent the next two years as a project engineer working with the city to carefully demolish this waterfront liability and eyesore. These years working in the middle of the city's financial district opened my eyes to a new industry, one that combined my passions for numbers and for working with people to achieve important goals. To educate myself, I enrolled in an MBA program at nearby Golden Gate University.

Upon completion of the demolition project, the San Francisco waterfront wasn't the only thing that had transformed. I began my finance career at Marin County-based Collins & Company. Fast-forward twenty-five years, and I am now the CEO and owner of Relevant Wealth Advisors. I have had the privilege of working with a select list of families and their foundations, helping them successfully navigate the financial markets to protect and grow their assets so they can confidently focus on their family goals and philanthropy.

You Don't Have to Fly Solo

In my spare time, I'm a private pilot. While I have the skills to fly solo, and often enjoy taking my plane up on my own, it's inherently risky to fly alone. As such, I frequently train with a flight instructor who has ten thousand hours under their belt, as opposed to my one thousand. Having an expert by my side while I'm in the pilot's seat affords me the chance to sharpen my skills and build up my own base of expertise—and their presence tends to be calming on days when the skies are rough.

A CIO is much like a flight instructor, providing that higher degree of expertise at your side while you navigate important decisions. The extra degree of knowledge a CIO provides is just as calming around the board table as an expert instructor is in the cockpit. This is especially true as foundations navigate economic cycles and changing investment climates.

The financial issues foundations have to contend with can be tricky, especially during tough or uncertain economic times. I have found that a voice of experience who can explain the bigger picture creates a more secure environment. This alleviates some of the stress and pressure that can accompany foundation business and allows all participants to unify around the same information.

My primary role is to be a calming voice that provides a basic framework, alleviates concerns, and delivers a realistic idea of what's coming down the pipeline in the current investment and economic environment. The most common question that arises in these situations is, "Are our investments going to go up or down?" Any financial advisor can tell you that volatility and risk are part and parcel of investing—period. The reality is, there will be times when a portfolio is down. When this happens, my role is to help clients understand why and educate them appropriately on how to react—helping them avoid making a decision in fear that may adversely affect their future.

Of course, there are families in which several members come preeducated about investing, so another thing to consider is at what level a CIO will need to educate. Some customization of messaging and counsel is required to ensure that everyone feels safe, aware of the facts, and cognizant of the plan ahead.

A note of caution: I've seen, more commonly than I'd like, that many CIOs choose not to engage at this level. They may not interact with foundation members beyond sending along the most recent investment reports. I believe this to be a missed opportunity. Everyone wins when the CIO makes it their business to be present, engaged, and wholly available to the needs of the foundation.

Navigating the Landscape of Family Foundations

I spend much of my professional life immersed in a culture of giving and gratitude. I am honored to be a part of that and to support the objectives of these organizations that are designed to leave a legacy of philanthropy. It feels good to know that my contributions have a real impact, both on the families I work with, and on the individuals and organizations their foundation touches. Few people are lucky enough to say this about their career.

I also know that the more obstacles a foundation is able to circumnavigate, the better the family's collaborative experience will be. These obstacles can be both logistical and emotional in nature. There are the logistics of making savvy investment decisions that abide by the regulations set forth for family foundations. There is also the stress that accompanies working within the confines of the regulations that govern family foundations, some of which are not particularly straightforward. Finally, there are the very emotional hurdles that can accompany working in a family setting, where family history and dynamics can come in to play.

In the pages that follow, I'll share some of the knowledge I've acquired throughout the course of my twenty-five-year career. I will shed light on regulations that aren't intuitive, share best practices for running a foundation and managing its investments, and provide some insight into how to create the best experience possible for all of the family members involved. Hopefully, this information will solve some of the challenges your foundation is facing so that you can rededicate your attention to what matters most—changing the world for the better through your generosity.

I Act as a Fiduciary for My Clients; That's Important

According to the Cornell Law Dictionary, "A fiduciary duty is the highest standard of care." It entails always acting in your client's best interest, even if doing so is contrary to yours. For me, this is a very important role—one I believe adds real value for my clients, and one I take very seriously.

As I work with clients, they receive my undivided loyalty and good faith. This avoids potential conflicts of interest that are common with investment professionals who represent a specific investment product or service.

CHAPTER ONE

WHY FAMILIES START FOUNDATIONS

With great wealth comes great responsibility.
—Bill Gates, founder of Bill & Melinda Gates Foundation

Bill and Melinda Gates currently run the largest family foundation in the world; as of 2017, their combined lifetime giving is in excess of $32 billion.

Incredibly, this is only the beginning of their generosity. Along with Warren Buffett and many others, in the 2010 Giving Pledge, the Gates vowed to donate the majority of their wealth to charitable causes, either in the course of their lives or following their death. With a total estimated fortune of $95.5 billion, the potential impact of their generosity is staggering. Already, the Gates Foundation has funded a wide variety of global health efforts, including research to treat diseases such as malaria, polio, AIDS, and tuberculosis. They have also supported significant overhauls in the United States education system, including providing schooling for the impoverished.

The Gates's lives are largely driven by their desire to change the world for the better and to positively impact social issues both close to home and abroad. In their foundation's 2018 annual letter, Melinda Gates divulged that she had recently been asked: "Why are you really giving your money away? *What's in it for you?*"

She replied, "By now, the foundation's work has become inseparable from who we are. We do the work because it's our life." Wow!

With the Gates Foundation Trust, Bill and Melinda Gates, along with Warren Buffett, take this selfless attitude one step further, with this promise:

> Because Bill, Melinda, and Warren believe the right approach is to focus the foundation's work in the 21st century, we will spend all of our resources within 20 years after Bill's and Melinda's deaths. In addition, Warren has stipulated that the proceeds from the Berkshire Hathaway shares he still owns upon his death are to be used for philanthropic purposes within 10 years after his estate has been settled.[1]

There's little doubt that you've heard of the Gates family and are, at least to some degree, aware of all the good work their foundation has facilitated over the years. Although the Gates Foundation is among the most visible of family foundations, they certainly aren't alone in their generosity. In fact, there are tens of thousands of family foundations of various sizes and endowments, which combined donate billions of dollars per year to charitable causes. In Marin County—where I work—alone, there are

1 "Who We Are: Foundation Trust," Bill & Melinda Gates Foundation, accessed July 25, 2019, *https://www.gatesfoundation.org/Who-We-Are/General-Information/Financials/Foundation-Trust*

more than two hundred family foundations. Despite the fact that you've never heard of most of them, these more anonymous foundations are also doing deeply meaningful and transformative work.

A Culture of Giving and Gratitude

We are lucky to live in a country that is ripe with opportunity. Around the world, America is known as the land of opportunity; our country is the place where everyone has the opportunity to achieve personal success. Because of this, many Americans tend to be entrepreneurial in nature.

Thanks to the tech boom and the tremendous wealth it has created, today more than ever before, individuals are deploying their excess personal assets to benefit both local and global issues.

Couple an entrepreneurial environment with the inherent kindness and generosity embedded in human nature, and it's no wonder that more family foundations exist in America than anywhere else in the world.

Accumulated wealth lies at the root of the good works funded by these foundations. In the absence of generosity and humility, such philanthropic acts would likely not be possible. Instead, excess wealth might simply be put toward funding a lavish lifestyle for the select few family members or saved for future generations. But wealth is not the only prerequisite for establishing a family foundation. A spirit of great generosity and a deep sense of gratitude are also necessary.

The generosity involved in family foundation work is straightforward. Family foundations are generally established by individuals who are dedicated to repaying society for the success they've enjoyed.

FOUNDATION NAME	ASSETS
Bill & Melinda Gates Foundation	$52,000,000,000
Ford Foundation	$14,000,000,000
J Paul Getty Trust	$13,000,000,000
Lilly Endowment Inc	$12,000,000,000
Robert Wood Johnson Foundation	$11,000,000,000
Foundation to Promote Open Society	$10,000,000,000
William & Flora Hewlett Foundation	$10,000,000,000
Bloomberg Family Foundation Inc	$8,000,000,000
W. K. Kellogg Foundation Trust-T/a 5315	$8,000,000,000
David & Lucile Packard Foundation	$7,000,000,000
John D. and Catherine T. MacArthur Foundation	$7,000,000,000
Gordon & Betty Moore Foundation	$7,000,000,000
Andrew W. Mellon Foundation	$7,000,000,000
The Leona & Harry Helmsley Charitable Trust	$6,000,000,000
Cronin Foundation	$5,000,000,000
Rockefeller Foundation	$5,000,000,000
The JPB Foundation	$4,000,000,000
Kresge Foundation	$4,000,000,000
California Endowment	$4,000,000,000
Walton Family Foundation Inc	$4,000,000,000
Open Society Institute	$4,000,000,000
Duke Endowment	$4,000,000,000
Carnegie Corporation of New York	$4,000,000,000
John Templeton Foundation	$4,000,000,000
Robert W Woodruff Foundation Inc	$3,000,000,000

Source: GuideStar

Perhaps less straightforward in all of this is the humility these families exemplify. At the heart of Bill and Melinda Gates's philanthropic philosophy is the core belief that every life has equal value. I've found this same belief also underlies most family foundations. Particularly for billionaires, this belief isn't necessarily innate or to be expected. There's a certain sense of humility within that mindset.

So, why are the founders of family foundations eager to give away all of this money? As Bill Gates explains it, "When life happens to bless you, you should use those gifts as well and wisely as you can."

A recent *Forbes* magazine article cited a study of 114 ultra-wealthy inheritors with a net worth of $100 million or more. The study found that most did not believe that their exceptional wealth placed them above others in society. In fact, they seem acutely aware of the role fate has played in making their vast fortunes possible. Nearly 90 percent reported the desire "to do something significant in the world." For many, this will take the form of philanthropy; more than 80 percent of study participants agreed that those who are wealthiest must also be the most charitable.

Of course, not everyone shares this philosophy—but many of the faces behind family foundations do. It is thanks to them that various organizations, communities, and individuals spanning the globe have been impacted in positive ways that might otherwise have been ignored.

The Age of Foundations

Today's foundations are thriving in a way we've never seen before thanks to the Information Age. We now live in a world where tremendous wealth is being created quickly, triggering even *more* generosity and *more* philanthropy as people become wealthy at a much younger age than ever before.

Consider this: if it takes fifty years to become a millionaire, you're not a millionaire for long. But if you hit the million-dollar mark when you're twenty-five, then you're likely going to be a millionaire for many decades. Combined with a robust global economy and attractive investment climate, your accumulated wealth will likely grow significantly over time. With a properly managed foundation, you and your wealth can do much more good over a longer span of time.

Giving back is now a top priority for young, wealthy philanthropists. In the San Francisco Bay Area, for example, I see a unique environment that much of the country has yet to experience when it comes to wealth accumulation. Young, wealthy tech entrepreneurs are making different lifestyle choices, and, as a result, philanthropy is becoming a top priority. Giving back is an important part of their core values.

Think about some of the estate homes that the Carnegies and Rockefellers built, and compare them to Facebook co-founder Mark Zuckerberg's relatively modest house in Palo Alto, California. This indicates a seismic shift in values. Mr. Zuckerberg could purchase any house he desires. He can easily afford the gilded lifestyle of our country's legacy philanthropists. Nonetheless, like many of his peers, Mr. Zuckerberg is redefining his own happiness and what is most important to him. Solving inequalities across the globe has become a new priority and the source of satisfaction.

Some people take this generosity for granted. When it's not your wealth or inheritance, it's easy enough to think, "Well, the family has plenty of money to fund their lifestyle for generations to live off of. Why *not* start a foundation, receive a tax break, and share the wealth?" This is easy to say—when it's not your money.

When it comes to money and wealth, there is often a tremendous amount of unspoken emotion. Even the most successful among us often worry about losing or outliving the wealth they've accumulated. Perhaps they know they have enough to live comfortably for the remainder of their lives, but what about their children and grandchildren? Or they worry that they haven't saved enough, no matter how much they have stashed away. What if they outlive their wealth? After all, we are all living longer and the cost of living even a modest lifestyle is increasing every year.

All of this is to say that it takes a special type of person to start a family foundation. Even a family like that of Bill and Melinda Gates, who have more than enough money to support several generations to come, could still find plenty of reasons *not* to participate in philanthropy.

Working with younger family members has allowed me to witness an interesting and welcome dynamic: their biggest concern about the longevity of their wealth is not how long *they* can live off of it, but how far they can stretch it for maximum philanthropic benefit.

Why Families Start Foundations

Beyond the generosity and sense of gratitude that underlies most family foundations, there are usually a couple of other key motivations to start these philanthropic pursuits. First, foundations are viewed as a family project. It facilitates bringing families together to work toward a common cause everyone can feel good about. Second, the founding generation often sees the foundation as a way of instilling philanthropic ideals into subsequent generations. Both of these are incredibly worthy goals and, certainly, two of the primary personal benefits family foundations offer.

Over the course of my career, I've come to realize that there are a few common underlying themes that motivate the establishment of most family foundations.

KINDNESS

One of the things I love most about my job is that it reaffirms my belief in the inherent goodness of humans. As we've already discussed, the possession of wealth alone is not enough motivation to undertake philanthropic work; for philanthropy to exist, wealth must be accompanied by a kind and compassionate disposition, as well as the aforementioned sense of gratitude and humility.

Particularly in this day and age, many might question the state of the human condition and how invested we really are in the well-being of others. Those people might be heartened to hear that a 2007 experiment by The Hebrew University of Journalism indicated that generosity actually exists on a gene—AVPR1a, to be exact. Additionally, research at the University of California, Los Angeles is pointing to the fact that altruism is hardwired into our brains.

At the end of the day, people start family foundations for the simple reason that they're nice.

Scientific research aside, I can personally attest to the fact that there are plenty of kind, invested, generous people out there. People who want to give to others and to the world simply because they can. People who want to make a difference.

Dress it up in whatever fancy term you choose but, at the end of the day, people start family foundations for the simple reason that they're nice, and they want to leave a cumulatively positive impact on the world.

LEGACY

People begin family foundations for any number of reasons, more than we can discuss here; however, the truth of the matter is that a family foundation often outlives the original grantor—or, in some cases, the entire family—that established it. Through the foundation, the family effectively leaves a legacy of philanthropy in their wake. This legacy can long outlast the people who acquired the wealth in the first place.

I currently advise a foundation in its third generation of trustees. While the husband and wife who established it are now deceased, the foundation has grown over time to a staff of seven employees, its assets have more than tripled, and it has evolved into a significant and institutional donor. The family that founded the foundation is no longer involved, but the foundation nonetheless lives on, achieving all of the goals the couple imagined during their lifetime.

For a more well-known foundation in this situation, look no further than the Ford Foundation, established in 1936 by a $25,000 gift from Henry and Edsel Ford. The foundation has far outlived its founders, and today is one of the largest international foundations in the world, with assets exceeding $12 billion. This results in annual giving of approximately $600 million per year.

Not only do family foundations create a legacy of giving, but they also establish a legacy of philanthropic practices to be passed down through the generations. It is rare to be able to continue instilling lessons about core values such as kindness, generosity, compassion, humility, and engagement in future generations beyond a person's life span. Family foundations provide a unique opportunity to do exactly this.

Furthermore, family foundations provide a wonderful reason to bring families together. As children grow older, move away, and establish families and careers of their own, it often becomes increasingly difficult to bring everyone together and to engage in a meaningful way. Family foundations provide a unique avenue for families to connect with purpose, and to work toward a shared goal. Properly managed, this process can be a deeply enriching experience.

COMMITMENT

It bears mentioning that, throughout the years, I've often seen families start foundations for one of the reasons we've discussed, only to find that they are motivated to continue giving for other reasons. For example, a family might initially decide to establish a foundation based on the tax benefits it offers, but come to discover that the greater motivation to continue comes from the way the foundation brings them together as a family unit.

Throughout the course of my career, I've noticed a very interesting phenomenon. While families have the legal right to close their foundation down at any point in time for any reason, in my experience, none of them choose to do so.

The reason is simple: it feels good to give. It is gratifying to effect positive change in whatever way and on whatever level. The philanthropic pursuits of family foundations often become deeply ingrained in the family's culture.

A Balance of Flexibility and Structure

Aside from the humanitarian and emotional reasons why family foundations stand the test of time, the way in which they are structured and regulated also comes into play. Family foundations offer a wonderful balance of structure and flexibility.

As legal entities, foundations must follow a required set of procedures and processes. These regulations ensure that everyone is forced to participate, which serves to invest family members in the foundation's endeavor on many different levels.

However, it is also important to have flexibility. While legal regulations and requirements exist, within that there is a tremendous amount of leeway in how those guidelines can be met. Families are given a lot of control in terms of how they run their foundation, and the foundation itself can evolve and shift gears over time as both the world and the individuals within the foundation change.

Family foundations offer a wonderful balance of structure and flexibility.

Foundations can give as little or as much funding as they want, as long as they gift 5 percent of their total assets per year as legally required by the IRS. Even within this, there is some flexibility. For example, if your foundation were to give away 10 percent this year, you could opt to give away zero the next. You can disperse all donated funds to one cause, or split it among a hundred different deserving entities.

There are no strict guidelines about what causes, people, or pursuits can or cannot be supported, as long as they fall within the government's regulations for a charity. You can give to food banks in America or education in Africa. All of this is left for the family to decide. Some foundations choose to stick with one very specific cause over the course of time. Others refocus their efforts on an annual basis. The flexibility to change the focus of support is particularly important for those foundations that have existed over the course of decades, such as the Rockefeller or Hewlett Packard Foundation. Social issues change over time, and, with this, it's important to many family foundation boards that their giving follows those causes that need it most at the moment.

Another wonderful area of flexibility within family foundation regulations is the fact that anybody can be on the board, including non-family members. This might include in-laws or even subject matter experts completely outside the scope of family.

Board members can change over time, too, as can the makeup of the board. One year, a foundation might have three board members; a few years later, it might expand to twenty.

The only irrevocable decision a family will make is the amount of money they gift to the foundation to fund philanthropic efforts. Once money is put into the foundation, the family can never take it back. From that moment forward, the gift legally belongs to the public. However, this doesn't mean that the foundation can't shut down—it simply means that all of the money must be allocated to charitable causes first.

Leveraging Your Legacy

Tax benefits may not be the most altruistic reason to begin a family foundation, but they are nonetheless a legitimate and valid consideration.

I often marvel at how clever the individuals who wrote the American tax code actually were. When you stop and think about it, tax benefits for charitable gifts of any variety are an incredibly thoughtful mechanism to promote philanthropy. The inherent generosity of humankind combined with the personal benefit of a charitable tax deduction creates an environment that supports the ongoing funding of family foundations.

The purpose of tax codes is to drive behavior, and the underlying goal of America's tax code is to allocate dollars toward those elements of society that need support, such as education, welfare, and social services. Other countries tax as much as 75 percent of citizens' income.

Their government then determines how that money will be allocated with little input from the people. The problem with this structure is that successful individuals tend to migrate away from those countries because, understandably, they want to make decisions about how their money is spent. People are often more generous in a country like America, where they're given the option to participate through incentivized vehicles such as family foundations, allowing them to choose when and how that money will be spent to address the issues most important to them.

This tendency to want to choose can be chalked up to human nature. For most of us, there is a big difference between being told to do something and being asked. We want the ability to make our own choices in all realms of life—especially when those choices involve the money we've worked so hard to accumulate. By funding foundations, people leverage their wealth with tax savings to maximize the value of their philanthropy.

Tax benefits through family foundations come in two forms. First, the person gifting the foundation typically receives a deduction of that amount for the current tax year. Second, the income grows essentially tax-free inside the foundation. These funds are also exempt from state and gift taxes. This means that these funds are worth far more in a foundation than they are as a gift or inheritance, where estate taxes could be applied at an approximately 40 percent effective tax rate.

These benefits apply to a variety of assets including cash, real estate, stocks, bonds, and mutual funds. Let's assume that you invested in Microsoft thirty years ago when the stock was trading at $1 per share, and today, the stock is worth $100 per share. If you were to sell your Microsoft investment as an individual with a $99 per share gain, you would pay approximately 20 percent of your earnings in federal taxes. In addition, you *also* have to pay state taxes, which would be another 10 percent cut in California, for example. When all is said and done, you will have lost approximately one-third of your investment through capital gains tax.

If you were to donate these same shares to a family foundation, however, and the foundation sold the stocks at $100 per share, the foundation would pay virtually no taxes. Almost the entire value of the Microsoft investment would be available for the foundation to invest or use toward grant making.

Of course, the tax benefits don't result in a net win for those motivated solely by the idea of paying less tax. If you earn $1 million, after normal income taxes are paid, you would retain approximately $600,000 for your own personal wealth. Six hundred thousand dollars in your pocket is obviously far more than the zero dollars you would keep if you put that money into a foundation.

At the end of the day, tax benefits are a great benefit of foundations—but they inherently must be coupled with a spirit of generosity or desire to effect positive change.

Making a Difference in a Way That Matters to You

Foundations are set up so that families can give to any charitable cause they find personally meaningful. This can mean anything from more obvious causes (such as education, the environment, and alleviating hunger) to causes that are much smaller in scope but nonetheless beneficial.

One of my favorite niche-cause foundations is the Stanley Smith Horticultural Trust, which was established in 1970 and is still funding projects nearly fifty years later.

Stanley Smith's wife, May, created the foundation upon her husband's death, to provide funding for education and research in horticulture. Horticulture mostly involves ornamental plants, rather than those that are developed for crops and eating. This narrowly focused funding is aligned with one of Stanley's lifelong passions, which was literally stopping to smell the roses (as well as orchids and other beautiful flowers). Stanley loved plants that are pleasing and enjoyable to experience, but which don't necessarily offer a great economic value.

The foundation isn't big, but it is very dedicated to its endeavor, and it makes a big impact through what may seem to be small measures: buying tractors for botanical gardens, funding signage along garden paths, and facilitating the implementation of irrigation systems.

While these gifts are quite focused and granular, they are incredibly important to botanical gardens, arboretums, and universities around the Americas and Australia. Most of the organizations that benefit from Smith's legacy are working on an extremely lean budget and, without the foundation's support, they would not have the resources to institute upgrades and perform necessary maintenance.

There is also a noteworthy trickle-down impact on the communities that enjoy the peaceful reprieve these gardens offer—something that is increasingly important in this age of connectedness and go, go, go. Smith's descendants have the satisfaction of knowing that his money is going toward a cause that he was passionate about and is positively impacting an area that was personally meaningful to him.

In a Nutshell

Whether large or small, granular or sweeping, foundations are run by uniquely generous people doing important work that impacts every sector of society and every corner of the world. Most family foundations are established with the intention of legacy and longevity, not tax breaks; a culture of generosity is the driving force behind these foundations.

In the chapters to follow, I'll show you strategies and tactics to help your family foundation meet its goals, to ensure that its funding is maximized, and to create an experience that is as smooth, effective, and gratifying as possible.

Just as it should be.

CHAPTER TWO

THE NUTS AND BOLTS OF FAMILY FOUNDATIONS

Every charitable act is a stepping stone toward heaven.

—Henry Ward Beecher

BEFORE WE DELVE INTO SPECIFIC STRATEGIES FOR SUCCESSFULLY RUNning your foundation, it's important to have a basic understanding of how foundations are designed and regulated. In this chapter, we'll look at some of the primary aspects, guidelines, and rules and regulations that will come into play throughout the course of this book.

A Detailed Definition of Foundations

Family foundations are legal entities that fall under the IRS tax code section 501(c)(3). They are usually funded by a single family member or couple, often as part of their estate plan. Most foundations are nonoperating and are therefore not "in the weeds" of running a nonprofit. In other words, the foundation does not actually run a food bank; instead, it provides grants to fund a food bank. The foundation does not directly develop a cure for cancer; it provides grants that fund the work of the American Cancer Society.

The money that a family uses to launch its foundation—its assets—is invested. When properly managed, those assets grow and appreciate, creating income. These assets are used to pay the foundation's grants, and fund its annual operating and administration expenses. It will also likely incur expenses for experts like CPAs and CIOs, in addition to regular basic business expenses.

Foundations typically try to run a lean business model. A typical foundation might have a small office and possibly employs few staff members, if they have any at all. Often, I see an executive director who acts like a CEO and is usually an employee. Board members are often not employees, but rather family members who volunteer their time. The one or two employees on staff do most of the work, depending on the size of the foundation, but a lot of expertise should be—and often is—outsourced. This involves things like bookkeeping, taxes, investments, and legal matters. All of these expenses are paid through the foundation's assets.

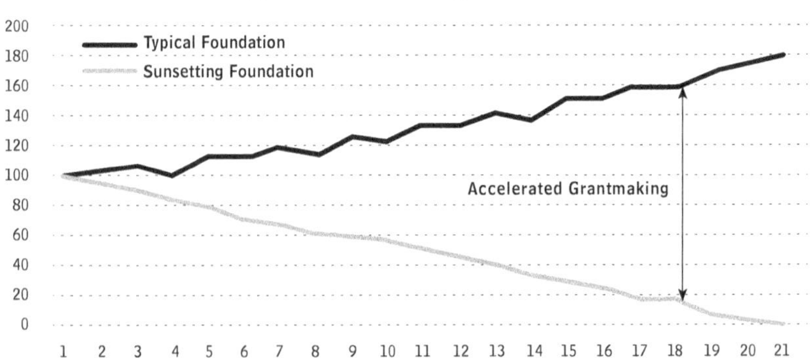

Foundations are legally obligated to distribute a minimum of 5 percent of their assets to philanthropic causes on an annual basis. This 5 percent is usually drawn from the income and appreciation the foundation has earned through its investments. That money is given in the form of grants for charitable purposes, rather than being allocated to the foundation's own charitable initiatives.

Occasionally, a foundation will want to make a big impact quickly, so it will have what is called a "sunset." In this instance, a foundation may decide that instead of awarding 5 percent of its assets each year, it will give away 20 percent or more. The foundation does this knowing that its portfolio will likely run out of money at this rate of giving.

From Family Members to Board Members

Most family foundation boards delegate their day-to-day foundation activities. They might also retain an outside investment professional, grants manager, bookkeeper, or CPA, allowing the board to keep their focus and function squarely on strategic decisions.

Although managing foundation business can be accomplished in many ways, most of the boards I work with meet between two and four times per year, either in person or via telephone or web conference. At these gatherings, they generally discuss the investment strategy of the foundation's assets and review existing and potential foundation grants. They may also discuss a variety of governance issues, such as board membership, tax filings, and financial audits.

Often, these meetings aren't that different from a typical board meeting, except they tend to be less collaborative. At a more standard business board meeting, most members are on equal footing, chosen to participate based on their experience and expertise. When it comes to family foundations, this is not necessarily the case. In addition to the general hierarchy that tends to come with all families, some members often have more business experience than others who may have less—or no business experience.

A well-defined grant-making process is essential to alleviate this discrepancy. It helps to ensure that *all* board members are engaged in the allocation of funds. This process should include criteria about the foundation's areas of focus, grant size, and how grants will be approved by the board. We'll explore this in more detail in chapter 5.

In the absence of a well-crafted, written grant policy, a few of the board members can end up controlling the entire grant process. This undermines one of the primary purposes of the foundation, which is to allow the entire board to engage equally in gifting the family's accumulated wealth to worthy and appropriate charities. Some foundations additionally alleviate this issue by allowing each board member to distribute a certain amount of funds at their own discretion. This core-satellite approach allows the bulk of the grants to be family gifts and a smaller portion to be individually directed. All of this remains within the family foundation framework.

How a Foundation Is Structured

There are two important aspects of a foundation's structure: irrevocability and public good.

First, foundations are irrevocable. This means that once money is put into a foundation, it can only be used for philanthropy. This rule applies regardless of what happens to a family's status, situation, or internal dynamics.

The irrevocable nature of foundations serves an important purpose: separating emotional elements from foundational operations. The money is designated for the foundation. You can invest it, you can manage it, and, most importantly, you can give it away over time. You just can't pull money back out of the foundation for personal benefit once it has been gifted to the foundation.

Second, a foundation's funds are used for public good, and with the IRS tax code section 501(c)(3) designation, they are considered to be tax-sheltered. This designation creates real benefits for a family who is interested in philanthropy—and, by extension, the public—especially when a liquidity event occurs in a privately owned business or a family has other appreciated assets.

Foundation assets are typically invested in a variety of asset classes, including stocks, bonds, real estate, cash, and other alternative assets (we'll discuss these in chapter 3). As these assets appreciate, the foundation will not be subject to ordinary income tax (up to 37 percent) or capital gains tax (typically 20 percent).

Instead, foundations pay an excise tax of between 1 and 2 percent on net investment income. In context, that is a nominal amount. The nearly tax-free nature of how these assets grow in a foundation's portfolio, coupled with the tax-sheltering benefits over a long period of time, cannot be understated.

The Current Regulatory Landscape

Foundations have experienced an increase in regulations as they operate in today's increasingly high-profile environment. Compliance requirements in every industry are getting more complex as regulations keep changing—that's the nature of the world we live in.

> Board members are held to a fiduciary standard and can be liable for improper or illegal activities.

It's more imperative than ever to ensure that your foundation operates efficiently and effectively, as board members are held to a fiduciary standard and can be liable for improper or illegal activities.

State and Federal Laws

State and federal laws govern foundations and, in many ways, the two jurisdictions overlap and are consistent.

Federal laws, however, can be confusing in terms of drawing the line between family and foundation activity (this practice is known as self-dealing, and we will discuss it in depth in chapter 7). For example, if family travel is involved for foundation business, it can be reimbursed as long as the travel specifically and clearly relates to the activities of the foundation.

To look at how regulations have tightened, let's take the example of a family that once held their annual foundation meeting in Hawaii. Everyone flew out to Maui once a year for a weeklong retreat, to relax as a family and discuss foundation activities. Years ago, this sort of activity was not uncommon. However, because the line has been tightened in terms of foundation versus family activity, this scenario would now be considered inappropriate.

Today, regulations require all expenses to be "reasonable and necessary." In other words, while travel like this isn't necessarily illegal, it is certainly ill-advised and may put your foundation under scrutiny. The state and federal government are strict about travel, and while meeting on the beach is definitely appealing, it's best to keep foundation activities more clearly defined.

Typically, the state supervises the activities of foundations. In California, for example, that regulating entity is the Department of Corporations. If this department identifies activities that seem inappropriate, it will govern the investigation.

States can and will also pass their own laws. For example, California passed the Nonprofit Integrity Act of 2004, which states that if a California foundation has more than $2 million in gross revenue, an independent audit must be performed on their financial statements. It also requires that books and records be kept in accordance with Generally Accepted Accounting Principles (GAAP) and that an independent audit committee oversee the audit.

This becomes tricky because a foundation can reach the $2 million gross revenue threshold by realizing gains or income that trigger a higher portfolio balance. The act allows a nine-month window for completing the required audit, which must happen by the end of the fiscal year. This can be an easily achieved, annual objective for an organized foundation, or it can be a huge distraction and obstacle in a case where the books and records are not current or up to GAAP standards.

For well-run foundations, these laws shouldn't present a challenge—they will simply act as a reminder that awareness of the rules and regulations of operating a foundation should be a priority.

A Foundation's Basic Regulatory Framework

The investments of most foundations are governed by the Uniform Prudent Management of Institutional Funds Act (UPMIFA). This legislation was passed by the National Conference of Commissioners on Uniform State Laws in July 2006. Since then, most states and the District of Columbia have passed this legislation. UPMIFA establishes a systematic framework for investing foundation assets. The guidelines have changed from what was once acceptable, and a foundation's investment managers need to be well in tune with these new guidelines.

There are three guiding principles of UPMIFA, detailed as follows.

DUTY OF CARE

The foundation's board must actively participate in the investment process. While each member needs to participate, this principle allows for the engagement of professionals should the foundation's board not possess those skills internally. In fact, most foundations work with one or more investment experts to ensure the foundation's assets are properly invested and the board meets its fiduciary obligation to protect the foundation's assets within the framework established by law. Some foundations elect to have a separate investment committee that reports to the board periodically.

DUTY OF LOYALTY

Board members must keep their focus on the best interests of the organization—this applies to both commonplace and commonsense interests. This means that, as a board member, you have a duty to make decisions about the foundation's activities based on what is in the best interest of the foundation alone. This can become complicated when the foundation's best interests don't necessarily align with the family's interests outside of the foundation. This important regulation emphasizes the separation of family activities from foundation activities.

DUTY OF OBEDIENCE

This may seem obvious, but the final principle is that family foundations must comply with all state and federal laws. I'm sure most of us have either accidentally or purposefully broken a law at some point in our lives without consequence. This might include something as simple as driving over the speed limit. Understand that foundation activities do not fall under this category.

In today's regulatory environment, foundations have a higher probability of either accidental or intentional misstep. Because of increased transparency, these mistakes are more visible than ever, and can easily be identified and lead to unfortunate consequences.

Understanding the Investment Process for Foundations

While we will discuss the foundation investment process in detail in the chapters that follow, it's important to have a basic understanding that foundations are designated a public status. This means that, while an individual or family can control and manage the foundation's assets, the money has essentially been permanently given to the public. Thus, the investment process for a foundation is designed to *protect* the assets rather than to maximize the return on investment—or even to just save money.

I usually explain this concept to my clients by relating it to the way most of them have found financial success. Some of the founders I work with created their wealth through a business that concentrated on doing or offering one product or service. They succeeded in their industry by that singular focus of doing one thing exceptionally well. They should be congratulated for their hard work, focus, and success.

A distinct mindset shift is required here. The formula these founders used to succeed in business is not the formula their foundation will need to achieve financial success. When a family funds their foundation, the goals are flipped. Yes, they want to grow their foundation's portfolio as they did with their business, but now they are legally mandated to diversify those assets to mitigate risk.

> Board members are now accountable for investment results, and also for the approach and strategies used.

An individual may amass personal wealth via speculation and excessive risk-taking. In the realm of managing a foundation's assets, however, speculation and excessive risk-taking are considered inappropriate. In fact, speculation is not allowed at all in a foundation setting. Board members are now accountable for investment results, and also for the approach and strategies used in this endeavor. If the results are bad but they had a sound strategy, they are typically in the clear. However, if the results are bad because they made inappropriate and uneducated decisions, the board and the foundation face very real liability.

This required diversification strategy creates a more successful outcome going forward, because foundation trustees can focus on a long-term investment strategy. The need to maintain proper diversification heightens the importance of having professionals managing the foundation's portfolio.

It is essential to remember that a foundation board has a fiduciary duty to manage all the activities of the foundation, including operations, awarding grants, and investing. Board members should consider delegating the investment management to investment experts—as a practice of prudence and as a way to ensure that best practices are employed. This also demonstrates to auditors that a board is practicing due diligence.

In a Nutshell

While foundations are designed to provide a nice amount of flexibility in their grant making, it is still important to be aware of the rules and regulations that govern the structure and operation of foundation activities. Understanding the parameters your foundation is operating within is critical to its long-term success and sustainability—not to mention its public image.

CHAPTER THREE

INVESTMENT FUNDAMENTALS

No one would remember the Good Samaritan if he'd only had good intentions—he had money as well.

—Margaret Thatcher

MOST FOUNDATIONS ARE STARTED WITH THE GOAL OF DOING GOOD IN society. Few—if any—are initiated because they offer an avenue or opportunity to focus on investing. Even if foundation members love investing in other areas of their life or business, chances are most are not bargaining on managing foundation investments as well.

Even if someone *did* start a foundation out of a love of investing, the investment of foundation assets is a very different process than investing personal assets. Much like I enjoy flying with an instructor—not because I can't do it on my own, but because I can learn about best practices and advance my knowledge—an expert can help you make the savviest decisions for your foundation's future.

As we've discussed, the moment you fund your foundation, those monies cease to be yours and become public property. With this comes the fiduciary duty to manage those investments to the greatest and best degree possible. According to foundation regulations, investments must be properly and carefully managed. This means that savvy investment of your foundation's funds is much more than a lofty goal—it's a priority and a necessity.

The Three Investment Structures

These days, foundations generally handle their investments in one of three ways: through a traditional, hybrid, or outsourced approach. In the following pages, we'll look at what each of these strategies looks like in practice and determine which will likely work best for your foundation.

The Traditional Approach

With the traditional approach, someone within the family handles the management of investments. That person may have a basic knowledge of investing and perhaps a background in business that created the family's wealth. Those attributes seem appropriate and attractive for such a responsibility. However, today they're just not enough to satisfy the needs of a foundation.

This approach is often seen when a family member has successfully managed their personal investments for their entire life and is using that expertise to manage their foundation's wealth. The problem with this approach is that the financial markets and regulatory requirements twenty years ago were different than they are today. You can't just buy a few stocks and throw them in a drawer, only to pull them out to look at every quarter.

Nonetheless, it's not uncommon to see foundations continue to follow this traditional approach. Although it is *possible* to have a good outcome with a traditional approach, the uncertainty of this process is one that I advise my clients to avoid.

The primary problem is that, without investment experience specific to a foundation, that individual isn't always able to function at the level of expertise a professional brings to the table. The person chosen to act as the investment manager may not be proficient in the different types of investments: stocks, bonds, alternative asset classes, real estate, and so on, which have varying characteristics and outcomes. If that investment manager is not trained in the complex nuances of these types of assets, they may not have the ability to make good investment decisions, especially when it comes to investing with diversification in mind.

Second, a foundation using this approach may lack the resources to track its investments adequately. With this, they can misunderstand the risk levels placed on the portfolio, as well as the performance calculations needed to properly manage growth. In the absence of this information, problems can arise that may hinder optimal portfolio performance.

Another challenge to the traditional approach is that it can create confusion among board members who do not have investment knowledge and experience. If the board lacks a professional who can educate them, they will not be able to act as a uniform team. A situation might arise in which board members simply agree with the individual handling all the investment matters because they have limited understanding or knowledge of the situation. This could lead to fragmented and unbalanced relationships on the board, which often stifles the positive collaborative environment necessary to promote ongoing successful growth.

> Having an internal person overseeing investments usually goes well—until it doesn't.

Investment management is a full-time business, not something that is easily accomplished in an hour per day. When family members try to take on the role of investment manager, they often struggle to provide adequate, timely reporting—an obligation in this role—because they don't have the time necessary to focus on investments.

Having an internal person overseeing investments usually goes well—until it doesn't. And when it doesn't, it creates serious trouble, sometimes even legal consequences. That's the risk a foundation takes when they don't partner with professionals. When something goes wrong, it can cause unwanted family stress and be quite time consuming, neither of which moves the foundation toward their ultimate goal of doing philanthropic work to maximum effect.

The Hybrid Approach

In a hybrid approach, the foundation board outsources their investment management to multiple advisors. Each advisor has a different area of expertise and manages assets within their specialty. It's not uncommon for a board to spread foundation assets among different investment managers, charging each of the managers with overseeing a part of the endowment. In this situation, board members realize they need to get investment experts involved to focus not only on portfolio performance, but also on the regulatory requirements of diversification.

While this approach is the first step toward working with professionals, ultimately, the foundation ends up without a comprehensive understanding of what is happening with its investments because of a lack of coordination.

Imagine you split the assets among five managers, each overseeing 20 percent of the endowment. Each manager will operate in their own silo, making investment decisions based on their 20 percent allocation, rather than the full 100 percent. Plus, it's highly unusual to have someone on a board with the expertise to consolidate the activity of multiple investment managers so that board members will understand the investment policy as a whole.

A hybrid approach—which often involves investment managers who might be friends with board members or the family—can also lead to possible conflicts of interest. This is an area that can create unwanted stress. While it doesn't necessarily represent a legal conflict, any hiring must be based on expertise and experience specifically within the realm of foundation investment management.

Reporting requirements are another area in which the hybrid approach often causes difficulties. When multiple managers are reporting on different areas of a portfolio, the board may receive mixed messages. Without a clear understanding of the risks placed on foundation assets when viewed as a whole, the investment performance necessary to achieve the board's desired goals can be less than optimal.

The Outsourced Approach

The outsourced approach involves bringing on an independent expert to partner with the board to manage the foundation investments as a team. This approach is increasingly common due to the mounting complexity of the investment landscape over the past several decades.

A new paradigm has recently emerged: the use of a professional CIO. The demands on boards to grow investment funds so foundations can continue to do the work they were founded for has fueled this shift. While the financial industry calls this "outsourcing," done properly, it's actually more of a partnership in practice. Partnering with a CIO brings numerous, extensive, meaningful, and valuable contributions to a foundation.

> Fundamentally, foundations aren't created to manage investments; they are meant to fund philanthropy.

Fundamentally, foundations aren't created to manage investments; they are meant to fund philanthropy, giving to causes that will make our world a better place. Partnering with a professional CIO allows the foundation's board to collectively and confidently manage the foundation assets so they can focus on their chosen mission. A CIO creates a single accountability point while avoiding the dynamic of choosing an investment manager among board members. With a CIO, the board is on equal standing with one another—an essential ingredient in operating a successful foundation.

To be successful in its philanthropic mission, a foundation needs to minimize stressful family dynamics. When using a traditional or hybrid approach to manage investments, troublesome situations can occur if one or two family members take on the role of investment manager. For instance, when the portfolio's performance is not meeting the board's expectations, it's in the best interest of the foundation to challenge the person managing the investments. A situation of this nature can be problematic when that person making those investments is a sibling or parent.

While you don't want to hurt anyone's feelings, as a board member, you have a fiduciary duty to call attention to any problems that may arise. This kind of awkward situation should be avoided because, once the tension starts, it's difficult to unwind.

The beauty of partnering with a professional CIO in this new paradigm is that they provide the solutions everyone wants, while avoiding the challenges of the other approaches. Unfortunately, boards may not realize the CIO solution even exists. Foundations that have been quietly doing their work for decades are often unaware that there's a better way to manage their investments.

It's also important to understand what partnering with a CIO *doesn't* mean. It doesn't mean that the board hands off the investment process entirely—just the opposite, in fact. A good CIO will educate the whole board on the basic character of the investment landscape and on the investments themselves, so that all of the board members have a better understanding of the strategy being employed. It is the board members' fiduciary obligation to make wise investment decisions for the foundation, with navigation help from the CIO.

Of course, a CIO will be paid for this work, which obviously represents an expense for the foundation. These investment managers are typically paid a percentage of the money they advise on. This rate is negotiable and might be as much as 1 percent of the foundation's portfolio or as little as 0.5 percent, paid on an annual basis.

Your foundation has significant assets, so even a small fee can represent a large sum paid to the CIO. If, for example, your foundation has $100 million in assets, you might pay your manager approximately $500,000 per year. If those assets increase, the CIO's salary will as well. However, perhaps more importantly, if those assets *decrease*, so too does the salary. This is a great system for the obvious reason that it incentivizes the professional to manage your money wisely. And, at the end of the day, while this sum may be large, the value an expert offers to foundations should far exceed their cost.

Last but certainly not least, partnering with a CIO who fully understands the regulatory environment will ensure legal compliance, while simultaneously keeping the board apprised of upcoming changes and trends in the industry. This provides the peace of mind that board members need to function at an optimum level of philanthropy.

Investing Foundation Assets

Once you have established who will be handling your investment decisions, it's time to set up your foundation's strategy. In chapter 2, we discussed the fact that one of the overriding guidelines for foundation investments is diversification. You'll remember that, in this way, personal investment and investing for your foundation are very different.

Rewind back to 1960, when investing was as simple as choosing some Pepsi and General Electric stock, along with a Bank of America bond. You would call your broker to ask a couple of questions and complete the transaction. Then you would let it ride. That was the end of that.

> Today, foundations have tens of thousands of investments to choose from.

Today, things aren't so simple. Foundations have tens of thousands of investments to choose from, including everything from mutual funds to individual stocks to private equity to real estate. It's difficult to wade through all of the options at your disposal and get an accurate, clear-cut idea of the ones that are best for the growth and security of your foundation.

Critical in this is that any money invested must be for the sole benefit of the foundation. In other words, it would not be appropriate to invest in real estate on behalf of the foundation, and then to allow your children to live on that property. Nor would it be permissible to invest foundation money in an office space that was used for family business outside of the foundation.

Both the IRS and most states have regulations that apply specifically to foundations. Some of these regulations extend to how those monies can and cannot be invested. This is important to understand to protect the nonprofit status of your foundation. Violating federal or state regulations can have real consequences.

Choosing Your Asset Classes Wisely

Each asset class has its own risk and rewards metrics, which are not always clear if you are only dabbling in the world of investing. Nonetheless, you must be aware of what these risks are and what they mean for your foundation. An investment expert can help you analyze and vet options from a knowledgeable, informed standpoint.

Due to the requirements of diversification, foundations need to tap into a variety of asset classes. Along with this, they need to understand how the combined return should play out over time.

The party responsible for overseeing your foundation's investments will first want to determine asset allocations. This will serve as an important part of your foundation's Investment Policy Statement (IPS), which we'll discuss in depth in the next chapter. For now, you need to know that the foundation board will set the asset allocation—establishing what percentage of the foundation's funding will be put into U.S. stocks, international stocks, fixed income, cash, and alternative assets. Creating this allocation strategy is by far the most important decision your foundation will make in the investment process because it determines potential future returns while mitigating risk.

Once your foundation has selected its allocation strategy, you (ideally working with your CIO) will pick specific investments within each category. While these investments may change either frequently or over time, the allocation strategy will typically remain the same.

Every investor wants the perfect investment—but that doesn't exist. Each asset class has a risk-return profile, which is why we spread money across them. There are a number of considerations for each asset, including risk and time. Let's take a look at the asset classes available to your foundation, and their various risks and rewards.

EQUITIES—AKA STOCKS

Publicly traded equities are an ideal investment for foundations with a five-year or longer time horizon. Five years is the optimal period to maximize your investment, but the beauty of investing in publicly traded equities is that if you change your mind about a specific investment, you can simply withdraw your money before that time period.

U.S. equities are the most popular asset class for foundations because, historically, they have provided excellent returns over time. Most foundations allocate approximately 40–50 percent of their investment funds to U.S. stocks.

The international equity market is bigger than the U.S. equity market; in fact, our stocks make up only 30 percent of the global stock market. International stocks include any public company that is headquartered outside of America, such as Volkswagen, Mercedes, and Alibaba.

Today, we have easy access to invest in international securities. Fifteen years ago, it was difficult to buy even Canadian stock—you had to go to Canada and invest in Canadian dollars. Many people feel (and, rightly so) that markets growing faster than America, such as China, Russia, and India, are essential to a diversified portfolio. However, international stocks are also riskier because we don't understand them as well and they also add currency risk. For these reasons, most foundations allocate 10–15 percent of their investments to international stock.

The purchase of low-cost mutual or exchange traded funds (ETFs) allows foundations efficient access to most any country, industry, or factor of interest, which means they can invest in a more diversified manner. Again, with thousands of choices, it is often challenging to identify which strategies are most appropriate for your foundation without the advice of an independent fiduciary.

FIXED INCOME

Fixed income securities, or bonds, typically provide between 2 and 8 percent income. Companies receive money by selling stocks and bonds to investors. A bond is basically a loan to a company, which provides income while protecting principal. Bonds offer a steady income but no growth on the principle. In the best-case scenario, a bond matures, and you receive the principal back.

The big upside is that when stock markets go down, bonds act as a cushion because they are stable and liquid. Most foundations allocate 25–30 percent of their investments to fixed income or bonds.

CASH

Cash is pretty straightforward. There is little return, but it never goes down and is always liquid. Foundations will want to have some funds available in cash to cover expenses. Most foundations allocate 3–5 percent of their funds to cash.

Alternative Asset Classes

While the previous asset classes are fairly straightforward, the alternative asset class is generally not so well understood. Alternative assets ideally perform like equity markets but have less volatility. Still, there are a few noteworthy areas of risk with alternative asset classes, including the fact that they generally require a time commitment, which means the funds are not liquid. Also, they are not always transparent. Most foundations allocate 15–20 percent of their investment to alternative asset classes.

In the last fifteen to twenty years, I've watched as more foundations chose to invest in alternative asset classes, such as hedge funds, private equity funds, and real estate investment trusts (REITs). These investment strategies can be quite compelling, but they are complex and need to be professionally managed.

Some of the relatively new strategies like hedge funds are sophisticated partnerships intended to lower the volatility of achieving attractive long-term returns. Private equity funds are another popular alternate strategy. These are typically invested in real estate, private companies, or other assets that have long-term commitments.

One of the biggest drawbacks to alternative asset classes is that their underlying investment process isn't always transparent. That may be fine, as long as it's understood that the hedge fund or private equity strategy is often designed to protect the methodology the manager is employing. This can make it challenging to fully understand the risk associated with a given strategy or how the strategy will perform going forward.

Fund managers typically try to define a strategy they feel is unique. As a result, they are often quite secretive about the ins and outs of their funds. Furthermore, the limited liquidity of these strategies needs to be understood so that, when they're incorporated into an overall investment plan, they don't cause a problem for the life of the foundation.

Let's look closely at two of the most popular alternative asset classes, hedge funds and private equity funds.

HEDGE FUNDS

The hedge fund model has some similarities to a mutual fund, such as being able to find out the value of the assets. However, hedge funds can do things mutual funds can't, like sell securities short and deploy sophisticated leveraged strategies to create extraordinary returns. With hedge funds, you will also have a defined schedule for liquidation, which outlines the time frame to withdraw funds. This is contrary to mutual funds, which typically allow daily liquidation.

The biggest difference between hedge funds and mutual funds is that a hedge fund is a legal partnership with covenants that protect all the partners—including your foundation. Somewhat counterintuitively, this can actually work to your disadvantage. If one of the partners in a fund decides to pull their money out, generally they can. However, if the fund's managers decide that pulling money would jeopardize the investments of the remaining partners, the liquidation request can be declined.

A hedge fund's legal structure is also complex. The bank arrangements that a fund uses to borrow money usually have covenants. These covenants can trigger a requirement for the fund to repay the bank if things go wrong or if the value of the fund assets drops significantly. During the 2008–2009 recession, hundreds of hedge funds went out of business because they borrowed money from the bank and, when the underlying assets dropped, the banks called in the loan. This can result in a total loss to investors.

PRIVATE EQUITY FUNDS

Another relatively new but popular asset class is private equity funds. These funds often require a commitment to invest a set amount of money for a period of time, typically between seven and ten years. During this time period, you cannot sell your investment in the fund. This can cause future liquidity issues in a foundation's portfolio if not considered properly.

If your foundation is interested in allocating a portion of your assets to private equity funds or other alternative assets, it's best practice to use a CIO with a broad understanding of these complex strategies. Your CIO will have a fiduciary responsibility to the board and the foundation to ensure that you have a full, unbiased understanding of these opportunities.

A representative from a hedge or private equity fund only represents the funds, and does not have that same fiduciary duty to your foundation. More importantly, they may withhold important information about their investment strategies that could negatively impact your foundation.

In the 2008–2009 financial crisis, many foundations were unaware of how their investments in alternative asset classes were actually being managed, which ended in catastrophic results.

Bernie "Made Off" with Foundations' Money

As the former nonexecutive chairman of NASDAQ, Bernie Madoff had an excellent reputation in the financial community and operated a substantial fund that attracted some of the most sophisticated investors in the world. Unfortunately, as we now know, his entire strategy was a Ponzi scheme. This was particularly bad news for many of the foundations who invested with him in the absence of a high standard of due diligence. Ultimately, their investments with Madoff were rendered worthless, almost overnight.

The Madoff scheme is a clear example of how foundations that dabble in alternative asset classes can get burned, even when the investment seems sound on the surface.

At the time, many foundations were invested in hedge funds that utilized a fund-to-fund strategy. With this strategy, rather than working with a hedge fund that makes its own investments, funds are invested in other secondary hedge funds. The idea behind this strategy was to achieve diversification and reduce volatility. The downside was that many foundations that invested in this strategy had no way of knowing that their hedge fund was invested in Bernie Madoff's Ponzi scheme.

Some of the clients I work with now, who invested in these kinds of funds before we met, are still waiting to see their money returned. I'm sure you can see why transparency in alternative asset classes is so vital.

One Size Does Not Fit All

One final thing to bear in mind when it comes to selecting asset classes for your foundation is that it is not a one-size-fits-all equation. You want to select the asset allocation that will best form the basis for *your* long-term investment strategy. Each asset class has a role to serve in the investment process, and a CIO can help you identify which ones should be represented in your foundation's portfolio.

Not all investments are created equal. Even within the same asset class, there are better, more attractive, or less risky investments. A CIO will have a deep understanding of all investment strategies, specific investment companies, and mutual fund companies. The U.S. stock market alone has more than twenty different types of funds: large cap, small cap, growth, income—the strategy options are endless for each asset class.

Some investment managers who represent these funds practice active management, while others believe a passive approach is better. The debate over the correct and most beneficial strategy continues to be waged throughout the financial industry. While approaches may differ, managers typically try to outperform an appropriate benchmark, such as the S&P 500 Index.

Foundations have a tremendous amount of flexibility when it comes to selecting the investment approach that will best serve its mission. A CIO can help sift through different funds and determine whether a fund has been invested with an active or passive approach. The ultimate objective is to assemble a comprehensive investment portfolio for the foundation with the goal of providing the highest returns at the lowest level of risk.

> Ultimately, the board is accountable for the investment outcome, so if they don't understand the basic investment strategy framework, they haven't met their fiduciary duty.

Determining the right allocation requires some strategic decision-making. An investment strategy for one foundation may not be right for another, so each foundation must tailor its strategy to meet its goals. A CIO will be able to offer insight to the board about what asset allocations other foundations have used with successful results. This advice will take into consideration the board members' comfort level with risk and understanding of the investment landscape.

Ultimately, the board is accountable for the investment outcome, so if they don't understand the basic investment strategy framework, they haven't met their fiduciary duty.

Investment Factors to Consider

While monitoring annual, weekly, daily, and intra-day stock market price fluctuations is an important element of investment optimization, other aspects exist too. The economic environment we're in is always changing, so it is critical to look at inflation or deflation and how economic cycles affect investments.

Unrelated Business Income Tax

Foundation boards also need to consider the tax consequences of investing. Your taxes are determined by the type of investments your foundation makes. If any investment could be viewed as a business, your foundation may be subject to what's referred to as Unrelated Business Income Tax (UBIT).

UBIT is normally quite substantial compared to the 1–2 percent tax most foundations are subject to. These potential problems are not always obvious or easy to spot. This is particularly true with alternative strategies because investments have complex approaches and the foundation is considered a partner in hedge and private equity funds.

The nature of those activities could trigger a UBIT. A CIO can help avoid such situations, and should be able to recognize a situation in which a foundation has invested in an entity that could be viewed as a business.

Your Overall Portfolio

Another investment factor for board members to understand is the role of *each* investment in the overall portfolio. This is a fundamental factor that often goes overlooked, because it is common for many foundations to have an individual board member managing the investments with several different advisors. This can work if that board member has prior experience managing complex portfolios, but someone needs to look at all of the investments collectively, including how each is allocated across different assets, and how each will perform as a whole.

Liquidity

As attractive as alternative investment strategies are, they are also, by nature, illiquid. Most people don't understand the value of liquidity until they need it. It only comes up as a tangible topic when things go wrong. Case in point, liquidity became a big problem during the 2008–2009 financial crisis as investors learned the hard way that the fine print of those contracts and partnership agreements allowed managers to withhold distributions in difficult times.

A CIO is very handy in discussions about liquidity because, as professionals, they have seen why it is so important. Foundation boards need to have a strong understanding of what portions of their portfolio are liquid and illiquid. This will tell them what money is available when markets are stressed.

When the next financial crisis rolls around (and it will), your foundation will want to have adequate liquidity to ensure that operations are not overly impacted.

In a Nutshell

In considering the regulatory landscape that foundations operate within, it is easy to see that, without proper guidance, even foundations with the best intentions can be left reeling from unforeseen investment missteps. The bottom line is this: your foundation's adherence to regulations must be beyond reproach. Without proper oversight of the legal and regulatory aspects of your foundation, the good work that you intend to do through your grants may be delayed or, even worse, shut down completely. Clearly, that is not an outcome any foundation wants to experience.

And finally, your board will be more confident adhering to a well-thought-out, long-term strategy when markets become volatile. They will know they are working with an experienced expert.

CHAPTER FOUR

MANAGING YOUR INVESTMENTS

Most people think that Americans are generous because we are rich. The truth is that we are rich, in significant part, because we are generous.

—Claire Gaudiani

SELECTING YOUR INVESTMENTS SO THAT YOUR FOUNDATION'S ASSETS are protected is only the first step in a long process. Just as important as making the right investment decisions is ensuring that these decisions remain in the foundation's best interests over time. Markets can be volatile, and they shift and transform—sometimes in the short-term, and sometimes over the long haul.

Either way, you need to understand where your investments stand at any given point. Just because an investment served your foundation's fiduciary obligation two years ago, doesn't mean it's still a good choice today. This is where investment management comes into play.

Investing is a dynamic process that continues to play itself out over time. It's important to understand that, although you may not frequently make changes to your portfolio, you should be monitoring and tracking it on a regular basis. Best fiduciary practices require frequent review, analysis, and reporting on all foundation investments.

In this chapter we'll look at some of the best practices for monitoring your foundation's investments, reporting on those investments, and being mindful about benchmarks.

Why Reporting Matters

Foundations are built to give back, and no one wants to give money without knowing if it has been useful. Establishing a thoughtful process to track the giving and its impact is a critical part of operating a foundation. These responsibilities take time and expertise.

When it comes to accounting, all foundations should adhere to generally accepted accounting principles. Just like a for-profit business, your foundation's tax returns need to be filed in a timely manner. Foundations also need to track and report on the performance of their investments.

Investment reporting serves two primary functions, the most obvious of which is monitoring the health of your investments.

Most foundations have a long-term investment horizon and will track the performance of their portfolios over one, three, five, and even ten years to analyze the long-term trends. As we saw in 2008 and 2009, foundations can lose as much as 50 percent of their funds in a short amount of time. For obvious reasons, this has quite an adverse effect on a foundation's long-term giving and sustainability.

While an individual may have a high risk tolerance and be willing to accept market fluctuations, foundations have a fiduciary duty to follow an investment strategy that is both diversified and appropriate. That's a tricky goal to accomplish.

Because of the regulatory environment, it is important that the investment process has a sound strategy for the expected return. First, and ideally, it provides a better return with the possibility of lower volatility. Second, it shows that the board has made a purposeful effort to understand the strategy risks and benefits, so that if something goes wrong, they cannot be accused of negligence.

A professional CIO can add real value here by helping to craft the Investment Policy Statement and working closely with the foundation board to set appropriate asset allocation targets (which we discussed in the previous chapter). The CIO should play an instrumental role in identifying attractive investments within each asset class. On an ongoing and frequent basis, your CIO will provide a consolidated report of your investments' performance. This simultaneously allows the foundation to focus on giving and leads to better investment outcomes. Investing is risky, complex, and even scary. These benefits will take a lot of stress off the foundation management.

Reporting also serves the more nebulous—but no less important—function of mitigating potentially detrimental family dynamics.

Reporting also serves the more nebulous—but no less important—function of mitigating potentially detrimental family dynamics.

Here is a common scenario: on a typical foundation board, there are generally at least a couple of financially savvy family members. Perhaps they owned a business, or maybe they studied finance. It might even more simply be the case that a family member enjoys reading *The Wall Street Journal* on a regular basis and has soaked up a lot of information that way.

Then, there are other board members who don't know a single thing about investing and are completely unprepared to make investment decisions. They may be more focused on giving and impact. Whatever it looks like, there is a wide range of investment expertise sitting around a single foundation table. I'm sure you can imagine what a disadvantage those less-financially savvy board members find themselves in when it comes to conversations about foundation investment.

Reporting is one way of bridging this gap, particularly when the reports are disseminated by an investment professional. An outside party can bring those who are less educated about financial matters up to speed, effectively creating a more level playing field. They can break down information in such a way that everyone around the table can formulate an educated opinion and, thus, have a voice.

Investment Policy Statement

Your foundation needs to have an Investment Policy Statement according to UPMIFA guidelines. You can view a sample IPS at *www.Relevant-Wealth.com/IPS.*

Foundations without an IPS in place will automatically raise a red flag with regulators, *even if all of their investments are faring well and meet regulatory standards.*

While the IPS has nothing to do with the actual performance of investments, it is a fundamental document that lays the framework for your foundation's investment process and describes how stakeholders will engage one another. Due to the ever-changing nature of a foundation's goals, the IPS should be reviewed annually by the foundation board.

Legality aside, the IPS serves as an important tool for your foundation.

It lays out your foundation's official investment strategy and the specific roles of key players, and it allows new board members to quickly get up to speed on the investment strategy. It establishes a process so that every single board member will have the opportunity to be equally heard and engaged.

The purpose of the IPS is to specify the expectations that should be met to stay current with both giving and expenses. It also specifies the life expectancy of the foundation, whether it intends to last forever or only for a short period of time. If the foundation is set up to last ten years, then it wants to give at a rate that exhausts funds by the end of that time frame. The IPS clarifies such matters. In short, the IPS provides strategy and consistency.

This IPS generally runs about fifteen pages, contains several straightforward elements, and *must* address a number of details. This includes three major components: total return investment approach, delegation of responsibilities, and investment diversification.

Total Return Investment Approach

A total return investment approach includes both the income and the appreciation of an investment portfolio to determine how the assets in total are growing or shrinking. It can also compare these results to the foundation's expenses to determine if the assets are stable, growing, or shrinking over time. Foundations need to gift approximately 5 percent of their assets every year for charitable purposes, while a smaller amount—as little as 1 percent—is usually allocated to other foundation expenses.

If a foundation typically spends 6 percent of its assets each year, this means the foundation needs to have an expected goal of earning a 6 percent or higher return on its investments to keep the total assets stable.

This would be reasonable for a foundation intending to maintain its size. Factoring in inflation would result in an increased return goal.

Delegation of Responsibilities

This part of the IPS contains exactly what you would expect it to: it sets forth how duties within the foundation will be distributed and who will make decisions.

A foundation may delegate investment and management functions. However, the board must exercise reasonable care, skill, and caution in selecting an agent. They also need to establish the scope and terms of the delegation. Finally, they need to periodically review the agent's actions in order to monitor performance and compliance. For these reasons, foundations should be leery of delegating investment responsibilities to anyone other than a professional. Delegating does not mean ignoring, and any delegation should be structured in a collaborative way.

Investment Diversification

A foundation might have a few fantastic investments in its portfolio that are performing extremely well, but that doesn't mean the foundation is in legal compliance. This section of the IPS lists the foundation's allocation of assets, as we discussed in the previous chapter.

This section of the IPS also ensures that, even if the board isn't tasked with the actual management of their portfolio, they will understand how assets are allocated, their performance, and even the nature of specific investments. An experienced investment professional will also be able to educate the board as to typical asset allocations for similar-sized foundations as well the risk/return profile of each asset class. With this, the board members meet their fiduciary duty of being educated and an active part of the process.

Portfolio Performance Reviews

Performance reviews are yet another part of the investment process that cannot be easily accomplished by an inexperienced individual. They require fairly sophisticated calculations that determine the total performance of all foundation assets. These performance reviews tell the board whether or not the foundation is meeting its objectives. Investment performance should be measured on an absolute and relative basis over a variety of time periods.

Investment performance should be measured on an absolute and relative basis over a variety of time periods.

It's important to understand that the goal of this process isn't to derive one specific number. Instead, the review takes a detailed look at each investment strategy to determine which ones are doing well compared to similar strategies. The board and CIO will use previously determined benchmarks in the IPS to make this assessment.

Benchmarks

Having access to your investments' performance isn't enough. You also have to measure that performance. This is done by comparing your results against a benchmark index that is reviewed on a regular basis. Benchmarks are critical and are often ignored as part of the investment process.

Benchmark indexes compare your foundation's total performance to an appropriate set of industry-standard benchmarks. These benchmarks often come in the form of an index associated with an asset class. For example, the most common benchmark for investing in the stock market is the S&P 500 Index. If foundations are invested in the stock market, they should compare their returns to this benchmark on a year-to-date basis, a one-year basis, a three-year basis, or a five-year basis. Although people are most familiar with the S&P 500 Index, hundreds of other benchmarks also exist for every type of asset class.

Let's say your equity portfolio is down 10 percent, but the stock market (S&P 500 Index) is down 15 percent. This is valuable information. Even though it's negative—you can still have confidence knowing that your assets are performing well given the investment environment. On the other hand, if all asset classes are appreciating in a bull market and your assets are appreciating below average, there's value to that information too.

The board then uses these benchmark numbers to determine whether their investments meet their set goals. You won't always exceed your benchmarks, but you want to come close most of the time. If that's not happening, it's important to adjust your goals or strategy as necessary, in order to keep the portfolio moving in the right direction.

Another important piece of information that performance reporting provides is determining the correct level of gifting. If portfolio performance is poor, the economy may also be struggling. You may want to adjust your philanthropic budget to ensure that the foundation isn't giving away more than it can afford. I've seen foundations give 8 percent or more in a down market where their assets were declining, and that seriously challenges the longevity of a foundation.

Benchmarking is nearly impossible to utilize correctly without the help of an expert because it requires significant data, systems, and expertise that the average person simply doesn't have. It's about much more than just reconciling statements and performance. Experts also understand how these benchmark calculations are made. You want to spend your time reviewing your results, not calculating them.

Rebalancing Your Portfolio

Rebalancing your portfolio is a dynamic process that should occur frequently to adjust to market fluctuations. This involves consistently monitoring your investment performance against your asset class allocation. For example, say your foundation allocated 40 percent of its assets to the U.S. stock market. Your stocks have risen, and you now have 46 percent of your assets in that asset class. You will want to reallocate this additional 6 percent to another asset class.

Actual allocation percentages are constantly changing, so the IPS creates a band around them. In other words, you may allocate 40 percent of your assets to U.S. stocks with a plus or minus 5 percent margin. Without this band, you would be adjusting asset classes all the time. These bands also act to set expectations about anticipated volatility and at what point action should be taken.

> Think of rebalancing your assets like a recipe. In general, you want to stick with the recipe instructions.

The process of rebalancing usually applies only to your liquid assets, such as stocks, bonds, and cash. Alternative asset classes generally require a longer-term commitment, so they are more difficult to shift around. This is another reason you want to be thoughtful in selecting your alternative assets like private equity and hedge funds. Fortunately, there are now many liquid alternative strategies that can be combined with less liquid strategies. This resolves this challenge while taking advantage of the long-term benefits of alternative strategies.

Think of rebalancing your assets like a recipe. In general, you want to stick with the recipe instructions; however, if you add too much flour to the bowl, you will need to readjust your other ingredients to balance it out.

A CIO should perform this rebalancing on a regular basis to make sure that you are hitting target allocations as described in IPS. They should then update you at least quarterly.

Legal and External Reporting Responsibilities

One of the great benefits of partnering with a CIO has little to do with investment, and that is protecting foundations and boards from accidental missteps. Even the most well-intentioned board may be unaware of the rules and regulations that govern foundations. That lack of information may lead to mistakes, which can lead to serious consequences—both personal and for the board itself. To guard against this, a CIO should oversee your foundation's nonprofit status by making sure the tax status is current and protected.

Even the most well-intentioned board may be unaware of the rules and regulations that govern foundations.

The CIO does this by annually reviewing the IPS. This review assures that one strategy or asset class isn't overly concentrated, even if it's doing exceptionally well. Unlike a personal will or trust, which are rarely reviewed or modified, an annual review of the IPS is often the best way for a foundation to confirm that external reporting is accurate and within legal guidelines.

Digital Reporting

Another often-overlooked benefit that a CIO brings to a foundation's board is helping to ensure that the board members have a clear picture of the economic climate they're in *at that moment*. That basic understanding of the economic cycles—along with a worldview of financial markets—helps a board see the impact those cycles have on asset allocation or investment strategy. A competent CIO is going to provide critical basic knowledge about why the investments are allocated as they are, how they should perform, and at what point those investments need to be changed.

A tremendous amount of data needs to be tracked to understand the swing of financial market changes on a day-to-day basis. A CIO should handle all of that tracking for you ideally on a real-time basis. A good CIO will then make that information available on digital apps or online so you always know where your foundation stands. The days of mailing monthly and quarterly reports are over. You can continue to live your life and attend to your duties outside of the foundation with the peace of mind that your investments are being taken care of.

The days of mailing monthly and quarterly reports are over. Having information readily available, anytime, anywhere, is a powerful and expected resource.

Digital reporting is becoming increasingly popular, as more traditional monthly and quarterly paper reports are no longer adequate. Having information readily available, anytime, anywhere, is a powerful and expected resource. For instance, our team at Relevant Wealth sends out electronic reports, hosts informative video conferences and webinars, and has a twenty-four-hour access portal so a board can see its investments on a daily real-time basis.

One of the leading software programs used by CIOs, including myself, is called Advent Black Diamond. This software tracks every transaction and asset class in a portfolio, every day. The information can then be delivered through an online portal, so board members have access to it whenever they want.

In a Nutshell

Unless you have the technology and resources to make complex calculations and comparisons to properly monitor your investment performance, you are left with few ways to effectively analyze whether your investments are doing well and if you will have assets to invest over the long term. Not only is this information required, but it is also critical to the health of your foundation.

CHAPTER FIVE

GRANT MAKING

No one is useless in this world
who lightens the burdens of another.
—Charles Dickens

GRANT MAKING IS THE ULTIMATE FUNCTION—AND, GENERALLY, THE appeal—of foundations. It is through the allocation of grants that foundations are able to achieve their ultimate goal of bettering individual lives, communities, and even the world.

The regulating powers have done a great job of ensuring there is an appealing degree of flexibility in the manner grants can be allocated. However, it's also important to understand that there are still rules and laws. It's critical that foundations understand the standards their grants must adhere to.

Unfortunately, some families with the very best of intentions assume that grant making is without parameters. After all, foundations are established on a voluntary basis and are nonprofit organizations. Nonetheless, the fact remains that once a foundation is established, it is considered a business. A family-run, nonprofit business, yes—but still a business. As such, there are some specific rules involving how grants are allocated and to whom they are given.

Focused Giving

So what cause should you give to?

Here's where some of that flexibility comes in to play. It is at the discretion of the family to identify what cause or causes it gives to. If a family has a specific interest in education, health, or the arts, the foundation's giving can focus on one of those areas. Alternately, the family may decide it wants to focus on a geographical area, such as their own community, so that a variety of local organizations benefit from the generosity of the foundation.

Deciding which organizations will receive grants is the main role of the foundation's board. And while the foundation may, for example, start out supporting organizations working in healthcare, the board might later decide to broaden its support to other areas. That's the power of a foundation; its strategy for giving to specific causes or areas isn't set in stone. Foundations have the flexibility to redirect their giving into areas and causes that its current board members find most compelling. This is one of the reasons so many foundations span many generations.

Example: The Ford Foundation

(From Capital Research Center's Foundation Watch)

The Ford Foundation's history can be divided into at least three phases. From 1960 to 1972, Ford was an empire builder. It strode the world like a colossus, and tried to remake America in the image of president McGeorge Bundy's can-do New Frontier liberalism.

In 1972, Ford began a retreat. Struggling to maintain funding levels during the 1972–1974 recession, Ford executives spent down its endowment, which fell from $3 billion to $2 billion. Programs stagnated and then were slashed. When Franklin Thomas succeeded Bundy as Ford president in 1979, his first task was to eliminate many of Bundy's favorite programs. Ford philanthropy became more obsessed by race and class issues. But the foundation's reaction to conservative advances was muted, and liberals who expected it to lead the opposition to the Reagan Administration were sorely disappointed.

In 1996 Susan Berresford became Ford president. She has done little to raise Ford's profile in the foundation world, and the recent recession caused Ford's endowment to take another billion-dollar hit, falling from $10.5 billion in 2001 to $9 billion in 2002. But even with this precipitous drop, Ford remains the second-largest foundation in America. Only the Bill & Melinda Gates Foundation is larger.

The Ford Foundation is a bundle of contradictions. For example, many of its grantees use Ford money to denounce the ravages of capitalism.

Grants

While foundations have almost limitless causes to support, the types of entities they lend their financial support to do have some limitations. For example, generally, grants must be awarded to nonprofits that qualify under the IRS tax code section 501(c)(3). Thankfully, hundreds of thousands of opportunities exist within this bucket for foundations to choose from.

There are two ways to identify which organizations deserve support. The first is to support organizations you are familiar with. This is a fairly common practice. It may be a university family members have attended, a local charitable organization, or a national organization you have enjoyed a long-term relationship with.

The second way is to use a grant application process. Grant applications help broaden a foundation's awareness of other organizations outside its usual sphere of influence. The grant application process typically has basic criteria defining the areas of focus that match the interests of the foundation. Generally, the application asks for details about how the organization will use the foundation's funding; financial statements showing the strength of the organization's finances; and, perhaps, some brief commentary about its leadership team.

Awarding and tracking grants can represent a significant workload—herein lies the bulk of a foundation's activities. When foundations use a grant application process, they have to review applications; decide how many organizations to support and at what financial level; track awarded grants to see how the funds were used; and, finally, ensure that all of the legal requirements around awarding the grants are met.

Midsized to large foundations commonly solicit grant applications and typically review them on a quarterly or semiannual basis; smaller foundations often award grants annually. Collecting and reviewing grant applications can be time consuming, and the process normally requires foundations to hire staff. These "Program Officers" identify the charities best suited for the foundation's investments based upon criteria established by the board.

When reviewing grant applications, foundations are looking to support qualified organizations that will use the money awarded to them in a way that will have the greatest impact on a specific cause. One important thing to note is that any organization with a direct material connection to the family is typically off-limits for funding. For example, as the Clintons and Trumps both showed us, even large, established foundations can find themselves in legal trouble.

"Feds received whistleblower evidence in 2017 alleging Clinton Foundation wrongdoing."
—*The Hill*, December 6, 2018

"Trump Foundation Will Dissolve, Accused of 'Shocking Pattern of Illegality'"
—*The New York Times*, December 18, 2018

International Grants

Foundation giving is not limited to the confines of the United States; you can also give to international organizations. With this, it's important to know there are certain restrictions around the types of organizations foundations can support abroad.

In the wake of 9/11, numerous requirements were implemented to ensure that foundations do not support terrorist organizations or other entities of that nature. This means that if your foundation supports an organization in another country, you must know how its funds are being used. By law, foundations are required to use due diligence to ensure they are not giving money to questionable causes. If your foundation wants to consider international grants, the safest choice is to give to IRS-recognized charities.

Foundation Grants Are Public Information

Many foundations are not aware that any grants made are disclosed via their annual 990PF tax return form, which is a public document. This means anyone can determine which organizations your foundation has supported, as well as the level of support you have provided. While this should in no way impact a family's interest in giving, it *does* mean that all gifts should be appropriate and follow the established regulatory guidelines.

Proper Due Diligence

The amount of due diligence involved in considering grant applications usually depends on the size and scale of the foundation. A small foundation may lack the resources to vet applications, so it might focus its giving on large, established, nationally recognized charities that provide some assurance and reporting.

Most foundations will give to organizations that maintain accurate financial statements and file annual tax returns. This provides the program officer some degree of assurance that the institution is managed well and financially solvent. Sometimes, program officers or other members of the foundation visit the charity being supported. Site visits allow for a deeper review of charity operations and also build a connection with the charity's staff and beneficiaries.

Foundation CIOs are usually not involved with the grant review process. Instead, the board should work with experts like the Council on Foundations (*www.cof.org*), Exponent Philanthropy (*www.exponentphilanthropy.org*), or the National Center for Family Philanthropy (*www.ncfp.org*). These national nonprofit organizations offer tremendous resources and information to help foundations operate efficiently, effectively, and within the law.

Collaborating with Other Foundations

While foundations are run like businesses, they do not compete against each other like for-profit businesses. In fact, foundations frequently collaborate on projects when a common interest exists.

For example, a smaller foundation might join forces with a larger foundation working within the same area of interest. Larger foundations typically have more resources and regularly share information to help smaller foundations leverage the success of their collective cause. This is a win-win situation because everyone is on the same team, pooling their resources to make a difference.

One of my favorite annual events is the Council on Foundations Leading Together conference. Once a year, foundations gather together to share information. Unlike business, which is driven by competition, nonprofit work is done by collaboration. Watching this happen in real time is a unique and inspiring experience. Foundations offer an incredible opportunity not only to collaborate with your inner circle to advance the common good, but also to be a part of something bigger.

In a Nutshell

Your foundation board members should enjoy the grant-making process. After all, it is your family's hard work that has provided you the opportunity to extend your generosity to causes you are invested in, both emotionally and financially.

One of the most disheartening aspects of my job is learning about foundations that, despite their best intentions, have experienced the ramifications of disobeying regulations, whether that results in a hit to their reputation or legal repercussions. Educate yourself about the parameters that apply to giving, and ensure that your grants are properly allocated and documented so your foundation never has to experience this unfortunate situation.

CHAPTER SIX

NAVIGATING FAMILY DYNAMICS

If you're in the luckiest one per cent of humanity, you owe it to the rest of humanity to think about the other 99 per cent.

—Warren Buffett

I WORK WITH A BAY AREA-BASED FOUNDATION WHOSE PATRIARCH'S four adult children live in far-flung locations around the world. Once a year, the entire family meets in person to discuss foundation business. One of the children travels from as far away as Switzerland—such is the critical importance of being in a room together to align on the foundation's goals and plan annually. And, as each of the patriarch's four children now have children of their own, the foundation meeting also serves as a special occasion for the family to gather for a reunion of sorts. It's a period of time, therefore, that I want to be sure isn't wasted in any way, so the family can spend quality time together.

As the CIO of the foundation, I consider it my responsibility to make sure this annual gathering is productive and enriching—especially with regard to the foundation's investment review. To do so, I keep each of the board members apprised of the foundation's investment strategy and performance on a monthly basis. This includes a brief activity recap, in conjunction with a comprehensive quarterly analysis. I also work closely with the chair of the board and foundation founder to prepare the board packet, which is a comprehensive document establishing the meeting agenda and including all relevant documents for discussion. It may seem simple, but this regular update procedure and cadence ensures that each of the board members arrives at the meeting up-to-date and ready to make decisions.

As a successful businessperson with decades of experience under his belt, the father knows how to run a business. He knows how to make quick, smart decisions. His adult children, though highly educated and successful in their own right, are used to their father making decisions, and therefore may not feel like equals as they sit around the table making decisions. After all, Dad is the one whose success has funded the foundation in the first place. This is a common scenario. My goal, therefore, is to provide more information and context when it comes to investment management beyond the technical, numbers-driven information included on the reports, so that even those who don't understand the numbers as well can participate equally.

Were my client's children to sit back and defer all decisions to their father, they would miss out on a real opportunity to make their foundation experience exciting, rewarding, and fun. A family foundation is an "optional" organization—participating on the board should be inherently rewarding.

Creating an Even Playing Field

Even with the best-laid plans, foundation dynamics can sometimes take on a life of their own. It's very difficult to leave long-established family dynamics and habits at the door, and to replace them with a neutral mindset totally removed from familial relationships. As an independent voice in these meetings, I am careful to treat each member equally. My presentations combine facts with subject-matter education so that everyone can participate in a meaningful way. Having even one neutral voice in a group goes a long way toward eliminating unintentionally biased dialogue, and ultimately, it makes the experience more enriching for everyone.

By acknowledging the complex relationship between parents and children (as well as sibling dynamics), a CIO can positively impact the levels of engagement and openness at these important meetings. By actively participating as an independent party, they can level the playing field as conversations about foundation business, finance, and logistics evolve.

This eliminates the hierarchy that may otherwise be present and, instead, allows for rich and dynamic conversations that allow every board member to participate equally. After all, this is the purpose of the meeting. If it weren't, the founder could simply write checks to philanthropic causes on their own accord.

Many family foundations struggle to operate transparently and efficiently. This is not a fault of the foundation members. It is simply human nature, and what often happens when we fuse together family and business. In the twenty-five-plus years I've worked in this field, I've noticed that the foundations whose individual members have the richest experience do more than just come together once a year to run down an agenda and discuss investment strategies, financial standing, and potential grants. They actively *engage*, regardless of their position with the family, and even regardless of unequal or disparate areas of knowledge and expertise. In this case, these meetings are more than just a gathering—they're a collaboration.

Most families desire this type of scenario, but it's not as easy as you might think to achieve. Unfortunately, in my experience, many foundation founders don't account for the challenges created by family dynamics and a shared history. Regardless of socioeconomic class, *all* families experience these challenges. In some instances these dynamics are more prevalent than others, but all of us can relate to the challenge of overcoming a lifetime of family experiences. First, though, we have to acknowledge that they exist.

In the coming pages, we'll examine some of the specific reasons why operating a family foundation can fail to be a gratifying endeavor for each and every family member. I will also share some of my favorite tools for ensuring that everyone walks away from the board table feeling engaged, fulfilled, and heard. In fact, you might even have fun in the process!

Family and the Business of Philanthropy

There inherently exists within family foundations a push-pull between the business of philanthropy and a family's established dynamics. It is absolutely possible to find the perfect balance between the two, but it often takes some effort to get there.

Over the years, I've seen many foundations err by overcorrecting and skewing too far toward running their philanthropic organization as a business. It makes sense: many of these families created the wealth that funded the foundation through a business. This means the founders often have a lot of business acumen. The problem is that it can result in the board experience becoming passive and something of a chore for other board members, rather than the rewarding experience it is intended to be.

Then, of course, there is the other end of the spectrum. As they sit around the board table, a family can easily lose sight of the fact that they are essentially running a business. In these scenarios, families bring the same dynamics to the board table they would to the dinner table. This might include power dynamics and resentments, both of which can bubble up and impact foundation discussions. When this happens, it's nearly impossible to make decisions based solely on the best interests of the foundation.

In both of these instances, it's the family that loses out. Society still benefits from the grants they are making. However, the family members miss out on the opportunity to come together and work collaboratively toward a greater good. Over the years, I've noticed there are a few touch-points that can be particularly difficult to navigate for the vast majority of families. Being aware of them going into your foundation work can go a long way toward a more enjoyable, productive experience for the entire family.

Money Is a Loaded Topic

Money is one of the most difficult subjects for people to talk about, especially among family members. It's interesting that in today's society we can have an open discourse about sex, politics—even religion—but money continues to be a largely taboo topic. Think about it: can you imagine a scenario in which you would be comfortable asking a friend or family member how much money they earn? I'm guessing the answer is a firm no.

The ability to openly discuss money and financial matters is one of the primary hurdles family foundations have to overcome. Remember, your foundation is essentially a business. And in business, money is one of the central and primary points of conversation. Profits and margins and bottom lines, maximizing revenue and minimizing cost—all of this has to be on the table for a business to be successful.

Of course, much as you might know this intellectually, treating foundation discussions about money purely as a matter of business can be easier said than done. Even if a family foundation *is* a business, it doesn't always feel like one when you're sitting around a table populated with the familiar faces of family members.

The Hurdles of Wealth

Money can be an even *touchier* subject when there's a lot of it, because it lies at the root of other difficult or potentially loaded topics. Even though the money allocated for the foundation is separate from any money set aside for inheritance, the existence of money in and of itself often impacts a family's interaction.

For example, if children know an inheritance is on the line, they may very well interact with their parents differently to avoid rocking the boat. It might feel like there's more at risk than it does for children in an average situation. In family foundations, this often means that children don't speak up about their own preferences or opinions, instead deferring to their parents.

It is generally expected that, ultimately, children will inherit their parents' accumulated wealth when they pass away. Most parents pass on their money with the intention of lessening the burden of and providing better opportunities for the next generation. This can become more complicated when a family has significant wealth.

Rather than helping their children or grandchildren get a better start, a large inheritance effectively makes work optional for future generations.

Ironically, it may decrease the odds of the benefactors doing the same type of work that was likely necessary to create the wealth in the first place. It might rob children of an experience that was instrumental in their parents' own personal development and larger sense of worth.

For this and other reasons, some parents might feel that a large inheritance will be more detrimental than helpful to their children's personal development. Parents may worry that their children will never learn the value of hard work, be truly motivated, or have the rewarding experience of accomplishment. Children in this scenario are often left hurt, confused, or angry. There was once an expectation in society that parents would leave any remaining money to their children when they passed away.

On top of the children's personal thoughts about a lack of inheritance, they may also be concerned about what others will think. What will it say about them that their parents decided there was a worthier recipient of the family's wealth than their own child?

The Giving Pledge

In 2010 Warren Buffet with Bill and Melinda Gates founded the Giving Pledge (*www.givingpledge.org*). The Giving Pledge is a voluntary and aspirational commitment by the world's wealthiest individuals and families to come together by dedicating the majority of their wealth to giving back. Total pledges now exceed $500 billion.

"This is about building on a wonderful tradition of philanthropy that will ultimately help the world become a much better place."

—Bill Gates

This giving "out" rather than giving "in" attitude speaks to a new paradigm in wealth transfer and family dynamics. Today there are over two hundred pledgers representing twenty-three countries.

Wealth is a powerful force that can be a wonderful blessing or the source of negative emotions, jealousy, and stress. These often-unaddressed undercurrents can create a lot of tension in families. That tension is easily exacerbated when they come together for a charity that was established with wealth that might otherwise have been bestowed upon the board participants. When this is the case, the foundation experience is usually not very gratifying for the family members. Not only this, but it also doesn't serve the best interests of the foundation. Tension inhibits—or altogether prevents—a truly open discourse.

It's easier said than done, but I always encourage my clients to face the situation head-on, and have a clear, honest, and detailed conversation with their children about their estate plan. Though estate plans are often fluid, communicating expectations about how an estate will be divided between family and philanthropy ensures that the stakeholders understand the motivation behind decisions.

A frank discussion can alleviate unnecessary tension, which paves the road for a more open and enjoyable foundation experience.

Stepping Outside Family Roles

While most of us approach business opportunities with an open mind, this mindset may not apply to family foundations. For better or worse, each individual involved brings with them an entire lifetime's worth of history interacting with one another.

While it's easy enough to advise board members to leave that history at the foundation door, it's not always so simple in practice. Even when family members walk in to a foundation meeting with every intention of leaving family dynamics behind, habitual behaviors are often so ingrained that they sneak into interactions without anyone being consciously aware of them.

In families, members tend to fall into set roles. Generally speaking, parents are the decision makers and have the final say. Sibling dynamics can go any number of ways. Siblings often clash; even those who don't fight have a long history with one another that may involve power dynamics. It can be hard enough to get siblings to agree on what topping to get on a pizza, let alone how to allocate hundreds of thousands, or even millions, of dollars to a long list of potentially worthy charities.

By the time we reach adulthood, these roles and dynamics are so embedded in us that they are difficult to change.

In many cases, it may not be necessary to alter family dynamics in the larger sense. They quite possibly serve your family perfectly well in more general scenarios. However, even overall healthy dynamics still might not be productive in the specific setting of a family foundation.

The most successful companies today are nimble and innovative. We see these qualities in their greatest expression within corporations that have embraced a nontraditional hierarchical structure. In this type of setting, everyone is equally encouraged to share their ideas and viewpoints. Obviously, this is a best-case scenario: everyone gets to feel ownership over the business at hand; and the business, in turn, benefits from a variety of people's expertise, experience, and viewpoints.

Establishing this sort of equality in a family setting requires intention. Inequalities can exist even in situations where family relationships are perfectly healthy—and even optimal—outside of the foundation. Consider a family in which the children want to please and honor their parents. This is an admirable quality that has likely been established by parents who have spent a lifetime earning the respect and love of their children. Outside of a foundation boardroom, this is a wonderful dynamic.

However, when this same dynamic is transferred into the family foundation, it means that children are likely to defer to their parents' viewpoints and decisions. With foundations, there is often an additional layer of subservience based on the fact that the foundation is generally funded by the parents' money. It can seem intuitive to give parents the final say.

> While deferring to parents or other leaders within the family won't necessarily destroy the foundation experience, it's a dynamic that doesn't breed open discussion, a feeling of equality, or fresh ideas.

While deferring to parents or other leaders within the family won't necessarily destroy the foundation experience, it's a dynamic that doesn't breed open discussion, a feeling of equality, or fresh ideas. What usually happens is that either one or both of the parents make a suggestion or decision about what the foundation should do in a given scenario, the rest of the family nods in agreement, and that's the end of that "discussion."

Generational Gaps

In some scenarios, this lack of engagement can swing in the other direction. Despite the rise in young wealthy entrepreneurs, foundations are still usually started by the elders in the family. They may be retired or at a point in life where they can relax a little and have plenty of time to dedicate to the foundation's activities and charitable acts.

Younger generations, on the other hand, are typically in a different situation. They may be at the height of their careers or steeped in the process of raising their own children, so the family foundation may not have the same priority for them as it does for parents or grandparents. Or perhaps they're simply not that invested in or excited by philanthropy yet. They may still be in the accumulation phase of life, focusing on saving money for their own retirement.

When any of these scenarios exist, families end up missing the gratification of actually *working* with one another in a collaborative way. Also, if the purpose of the foundation is to teach younger generations about philanthropy, they're not necessarily learning much through a process they don't have the freedom or motivation to truly engage or invest in.

Alleviating Innate Behaviors

Such situations require a proactive approach that acknowledges family dynamics and ensures that they do not inhibit the mission of the foundation. In fact, I've seen families seize their interaction in foundation work as a means of healing other problems and coming together in new ways. It feels good to do good; that's simply human nature. When each family member plays an important role *and* they are part of a collective working toward a shared goal, it is an incredibly rewarding and transformative experience.

For this to happen, the person who has the lion's share of the power within the family has to acknowledge and address the imbalance and potentially varied levels of interest in the foundation. This involves making a concerted effort to engage other family members in a positive and meaningful way. It requires managing meetings and discussions so that they involve each person around the table in equal measure. With this, I often advise families to have a formal vote so that everyone feels like they are part of the process and their preferences are being heard.

The Wealth-Happiness Paradox

Who wants to be a millionaire? For many people, the desire to increase their wealth is a lifelong goal. From a young age, we're taught to accumulate, save, and invest. This process is supposed to make us happier. But does it? You may be surprised to learn that wealth can often derail our happiness.

UC Davis psychologist Robert Emmons observes, "The correlation between income and happiness is positive but modest. Money buys happiness, but it buys less of it than most people think." On the other hand, he says, "Filling a grocery bag for someone else rather than purchasing a coveted designer bag for yourself is a promising route to lasting happiness." If Emmons is to be believed, it seems like we might be missing something in our quest for happiness.

Extensive research now tells us that the key to being happy is to find gratitude for both the big and small things in our life today. In other words, we need to live in the now and stop focusing on—or agonizing about—the future. This attitude of gratitude pays huge and immediate dividends.

Of course, it is possible to be wealthy and happy, but only if you acknowledge the responsibility that comes with having money and avoid actions that sabotage happiness. The good news is that there are positive, proactive steps you can take to protect both your wealth and your happiness. To start, you should be on guard for some common pitfalls.

1. **Poor communication:** A lack of communication can leave us unprepared for the potentially negative consequences of having money. "You'd be surprised how rarely affluent couples discuss their wealth," says David Fink, a leading San Francisco-based divorce arbitrator. "It used to be considered rude to discuss finances, but discussing your feelings about money can lead to healthier relationships."

2. **Taking money for granted:** A stick of dynamite in your hand will get your attention because of its destructive power. Wealth can be just as powerful and harmful—especially when you take your

wealth for granted. Remember that most friends and family of wealthy people are often not wealthy. It's essential to appreciate the perspective of those in different financial circumstances. Ignoring this can lead to isolation. Begin by asking yourself what you would do in a particular situation if you weren't wealthy. Money is a great tool and resource, but it can be destructive when it skews your personal attitudes or behavior.

3. **Keeping money a secret from your heirs:** Passing wealth to heirs is often done in secrecy because parents worry their children will be negatively affected by the gift. The reality is that poor communication can lead to stress, anger, and confusion. Being honest with heirs ensures that there is no confusion about your intentions and prevents misunderstandings as time passes. If you plan to pass your wealth on to friends or family, let them know. This gives them time to absorb how this gift will affect their life. Also, making random, piecemeal gifts with little notice may seem generous, but it can actually send mixed messages. Instead, consider making consistent gifts over time. Tell the recipients they can expect the gifts with no strings attached. After all, this is what makes a gift, a gift. Expect and ask for nothing in return.

4. **Giving children unequal gifts:** Even with the best of intentions, giving money to family members can backfire. One common mistake is to make bigger or more frequent gifts to those with more perceived needs. If you have four children, make the same gift to all of them, regardless of their individual needs. Why punish those who are more financially successful? We all know the value of raising children without playing favorites. Making financial gifts is no different.

5. **Mixing business and pleasure:** Wealth management can be a very personal and very emotional process. It should generally remain separate from other personal aspects of our lives. The management of your wealth should be handled with a professional, businesslike approach. Discussing personal financial matters with friends or family in social settings can often derail those relationships and special times. Consider your wealth management a key priority. Working with seasoned professionals you trust will help you move confidently through your life without the need to involve friends and family in your personal finances.

6. **Trying to buy love and gratitude:** Too often, gifts are given with strings attached. Estate plans often include a number of provisions limiting, reducing, controlling, and even preventing gifts based on the behavior of the recipient. Worse, control is sometimes never passed down to the recipients. They continue to be treated like children in perpetuity. Clearly, some caution is appropriate when planning irrevocable gifts, but a true gift should be a one-sided transaction. Research has shown that true happiness is derived through gratitude. Be gracious with your giving and acknowledge how fortunate you are to be in a position to give. This will magnify the benefit both to you and the recipient. Combining gratitude with a "no strings attached" attitude will most likely create your desired outcome.

7. **Assuming special treatment:** If you are wealthy, it can be easy to think, "I'm rich, so I'm special." No, actually, you're just rich. You may be special, but being rich does not entitle you to special treatment. It might allow you to *purchase* special treatment, but you're not entitled to it. Some wealthy individuals overlook this detail and become irritated when they are not granted special

treatment. This might be the single greatest impediment to happiness. In seeking validation and acknowledgment, individuals often act in a way that creates resentment and leads to isolation. Instead of being entitled, be gracious. This is one of the biggest keys to making your life truly rich and special.

There are certainly greater problems in life than being wealthy. However, both common sense and research tell us that money alone doesn't buy happiness. If you're lucky enough to have found financial prosperity, it's a good idea to have a comprehensive plan and a grounded attitude to ensure that your wealth doesn't derail your happiness. When developing your plan, you should also consider how money impacts your personal relationships. Understanding your values, communicating those values with your family, and living those values in your daily life are key ingredients for a happier life.

Bringing in a Third Party

In my experience, the most successful and fulfilling family foundations incorporate a team of outside experts to help the family maximize the success of their foundation. Depending on the size and scope of the foundation, this may be a handful of people—who split running the operations side of the foundation, investment, reporting, and grant analysis—or it may be a single person, such as an executive director, who handles some or all of these tasks.

Incorporating a Neutral Voice

It can help to have a third party present at foundation meetings—whether it's the executive director or another professional—to act as a mediator. This neutral party helps ensure that everyone has an equal opportunity to add their voice and opinions to the conversation. It also ensures that the meeting stays on track and addresses the agenda in a thoughtful and timely manner. With this, the foundation becomes a truly collaborative group effort, rather than a process of simply voting with the family member in charge or along other division lines.

Removing these obstacles better allows families to engage in a rich, collaborative, and personally rewarding experience by focusing their limited time together on strategic decisions without the distraction of dynamics. It also alleviates the minutia, which allows family members with full-time lives outside of their foundation to fulfill their fiduciary duty of being a board member while still leading the life of their choosing. When done properly, family members can simply look forward to the fun, collaborative part of the philanthropy process.

In a Nutshell

Sometimes, when families are stuck in the mire of decision-making and operations, even the founders start to forget why they began their foundation in the first place. Whenever I speak to someone in this position, I remind them that there is no law dictating they run a family foundation. They can just as easily—and, in fact, probably much *more* easily—write a check to their favorite charities, and that will be the end of it. But that's not what they really want to do.

Foundations offer the opportunity for a shared family experience. They can bring otherwise removed families living their own separate lives back together for a common cause. They teach younger generations about the importance of being of service and a good local and global citizen. Family dynamics can sometimes be tricky to navigate, yes, but it's worth the effort. Of all the investments you've ever made for your family, this one might just be the most valuable.

CHAPTER SEVEN

AVOIDING COMMON MISTAKES

Learn from the mistakes of others.
You can't live long enough to make them all yourself.
—Eleanor Roosevelt

California law requires that an independent audit be performed if your foundation earns more than $2 million in a year. Contracting an auditor costs approximately $20,000. For this price, the auditor scours through foundation records and creates a document that is usually filed away in the foundation archives and never seen again. Nonetheless, performing this audit is not optional for California family foundations. Failing to do so could come back to haunt you.

California law requires that an independent audit be performed if your foundation earns more than $2 million in a year.

If it is discovered that a foundation did not perform this mandatory audit, the audit will have to be done retroactively. This would flag a regulatory review. Much as is the case with an IRS audit, once a foundation is flagged, the door to scrutiny opens wide and an arduous process ensues.

No foundation wants to be under review. It isn't good for the family's reputation, and fines are often associated even with inadvertent mistakes. Each board member is responsible for the foundation, so there may be some personal liability as well. As with any other board situation, the idea of responsibility for an entity larger than yourself can seem nebulous until it actually impacts you in a material way.

In addition to the federal laws that govern foundations, every state has its own laws as well, much like California has this audit requirement. These laws and regulations can seem like busywork or even downright silly, but they still have to be adhered to. Often, foundations aren't even aware many of these laws exist. But they do, and they're important. That's just one of the reasons why a collaborative effort is so important—it helps to ensure that nothing falls through the cracks.

Due to the nature of family foundations, it can be easy to forget that foundation work is more than just a family project or endeavor. As you now well know, foundations represent much more than that and are subject to a variety of regulations.

Whereas the majority of regulations we've discussed throughout the course of this book so far are fairly intuitive, many others are not. It can be dangerously easy to err in the eyes of the law, even when your intentions are pure. Following are some tips for avoiding stressful and potentially damaging and embarrassing situations.

Running a Private Foundation in a Public World

Today's foundations are faced with a smaller margin of error than ever before, which means that board members face obstacles that Carnegie and Rockefeller never had to contend with.

Although the IRS refers to family foundations as private foundations, the reality is there is nothing private about them in practice. In the past, when foundations made an innocent error, no one was ever the wiser; the foundation adjusted and went on with business as usual. All too often, this is not the case in today's transparent climate.

Today, much of the information about your foundation is public. Because of ever-increasing digital access, your foundation is open to public scrutiny that can damage your family's reputation. As we all know, news travels quickly and can be distorted in the process.

I am saddened when I see a foundation land in the public eye as a result of mistakes that are common but, nonetheless, blown up into a media storm. No matter how innocent the foundation may be, the truth of the matter is that this sort of negative press is almost impossible to reverse. Bad publicity can have a significantly negative impact on the family, their foundation, and all of the charitable causes the foundation supports.

Families start foundations to have a positive influence on their community and the world. They want to leverage the family name for good works. Bad publicity runs in the face of this. Even when that publicity is inaccurate, foundations can still be deeply impacted.

For the past two years, the attorney general has been investigating the Donald J. Trump Foundation for self-dealing. Self-dealing is a term the IRS uses to refer to the practice of using foundation assets to benefit the family behind the foundation.

President Trump hasn't been sued—after all, this matter is only in the investigation stage. However, this sensational news has been blasted across most media outlets, including the front page of *The New York*

Times. Whether it's true or not, the investigation has given Trump's foundation a bad name. In fact, I'm willing to guess you've already formed your own opinions about the Trump family's guilt or lack thereof in the course of reading the last couple of paragraphs.

At the time of writing this book, we still don't know if the Trump family is guilty or not, or how this case is going to play out. In the meantime, the foundation's reputation has been shredded to the point where the foundation was dissolved at the end of last year.

The Trump family is somewhat extenuating because most people have already formulated opinions about them. However, this sort of situation is damaging for any family foundation, regardless of how well known the family is. Damage is usually not limited to the foundation itself, because most foundations bear the name of the family behind them. The family reputation takes a hit as well.

Even in cases where investigations don't turn up any wrongdoing, any scrutiny is still detrimental. It's also an expensive process, regardless of the outcome. These situations can take on a life of their own and be drawn out for more than a decade once investigations, litigation, and appeals are all said and done.

Investigations aren't always fair. Some people have ulterior motives in identifying mistakes. They have their own political or personal agenda that has nothing to do with your foundation. Going back to the Trump example, my guess is that if he weren't the president of the United States, this investigation wouldn't be happening.

Most foundations are quietly doing meaningful work with the best of intentions. Ninety-nine percent of the time, foundations are established in a thoughtful way by generous people. When you get down to it, there aren't a lot of stories about foundations doing bad things, because most of these families are thoughtful, professional, and well-intentioned. In the best way, they're actually pretty boring.

All of this is why it's so important to understand some of the more common ways family foundations unwittingly stumble. Following are five of the mistakes I see most frequently, all of which are easily avoided.

Self-Dealing

As we discussed in the previous section, self-dealing is when families use foundations to benefit their personal cause. This includes not only the family that established the foundation, but also any people and entities closely associated with the foundation. They too are disqualified from benefitting from the foundation in any sort of monetary way, including through the provision of goods and services. Officers, directors, board members, family members, and any affiliated businesses are all included in this category.

In short, if a board member, attorney, corporate officer, or any other fiduciary—known as disqualified persons—takes advantage of their position in a foundation transaction and acts in their own best interest instead of in the interest of the foundation, it opens the door to penalties for these serious infractions. This sounds pretty straightforward, but it involves much more than writing out a check to a disqualified person. Self-dealing can also include utilizing *any* type of foundation resources in a manner that can be construed as benefitting disqualified persons or entities.

The IRS considers the following transactions as acts of self-dealing between a private foundation and a disqualified person:

- Sale, exchange, or leasing of property
- Lending money or other extensions of credit
- Providing goods, services, or facilities
- Paying compensation or reimbursing expenses to a disqualified person
- Transferring foundation income or assets to, or for the use or benefit of, a disqualified person
- Certain agreements to make payments of money or property to government officials
- Transactions between organizations controlled by a private foundation may also be self-dealing.

Let's say, for instance, that an officer decides to loan the family business money from the family foundation. No matter how quickly the foundation money is reimbursed or the interest rate paid, this practice is strictly prohibited.

A potentially sticky area of self-dealing comes in instances when family foundations decide to hire family members to run the foundation. This practice is not uncommon, and it's perfectly legal. In fact, I work with several foundations that compensate family members who have been hired to run various facets of the foundation. However, in this instance, the family member's compensation must be considered reasonable and appropriate for their role based on reputable sources, such as independent industry surveys. It must be ensured and documented that the disqualified person is being paid the same rate for the same services that a similarly qualified person would be for that work.

These regulations apply to foundation donors as well. It is also considered self-dealing when a "substantial contributor," or someone who has made a large gift to the foundation, is then hired on for their services or expertise. This can be a bit of a gray area because there are instances where a donor's services can be purchased on behalf of the foundation. All of this is determined on a case-by-case basis, so it's important to run any situations that fall into a gray area by an expert. In cases like this, you are always better safe than sorry.

To guard against self-dealing, foundations should document any professional relationship they may have with a person or entity that is considered disqualified. This includes executing written contracts that describe both the services being provided and the compensation. Such documentation should be handled by a trusted advisor, such as the foundation's CIO, accounting firm, or auditor.

One final note on self-dealing: even in cases in which a family foundation is completely on the right side of regulations, the public might have a certain perception about foundations that compensate family members for their work. This is one area where the accessibility of foundation information can actually work on behalf of the family. On the 990PF tax return, foundations are required to log how many hours an employee is working, along with their compensation. This means the public can see for themselves how a family member is compensated as compared to anyone else.

Sharing Resources

Sharing resources is a common area where foundations come under fire, for this very logical reason: many families who run a foundation also run a business. From a practical point of view, it may make sense to house both of these entities in a single office, or to allocate a portion of the business office to foundation works.

Let's say I already have an office that I run my business out of. Instead of renting a separate office for my foundation, I decide it makes more sense to house the foundation in one of my office suites. That way, I'm right down the hall, readily available to take care of foundation business as it arises. I calculate that the foundation is using 10 percent of my total office space, so I charge that amount to the foundation for rent reimbursement.

While this might seem practical, it's prohibited. To meet regulatory standards, the foundation would have to pay their portion of the rent directly to the landlord. It should also have its own lease agreement.

All of this seems like minutia and, in many ways, it is. Which is precisely why the regulations around sharing resources can get so sticky.

Much as is the case with self-dealing, when it comes to sharing resources, any comingling between business and foundation resources must occur as an arm's-length transaction.

Investment-Related Mistakes

We've already discussed investment strategies in depth. However, they bear mentioning again here, because it's important to understand that investment is one of the areas in which family foundations tend to falter most frequently.

It's critical to understand that family foundations have a fiduciary duty to understand their investment process. This doesn't mean you have to be an expert yourself. It *does* mean that if you're not an expert, you are obligated to work with one.

Family foundations are highly regulated. Many foundations make investment-related mistakes simply because they don't understand the specifics of those regulations until they accidentally violate them.

A professional financial consultant should provide foundations with the understanding they need pertaining to their responsibilities as board members and, ultimately, as fiduciaries. They should ensure that you are provided with professional investment advice and, within that, adhere to all regulations that may restrict your investment strategies. At a minimum, all foundations must have a written IPS that specifies their investment process.

Within all of these requirements, there is room for flexibility. An expert will be able to specify best practices for your foundation based on your particular goals and risk tolerance, while keeping regulatory requirements in mind.

Personal Pledges

Let's say that my wife and I go to a fundraising event for my child's school. Obviously, this is a cause we care about deeply and are emotionally invested in. While there, I make a pledge to donate $10,000 to be put toward the school's new science building. Feeling great, I go home and write the check out from my family foundation.

Why is this illegal, if my foundation has a vested interest in the school and likely would have agreed to contribute the same amount of money to the same cause? Well, it's because this type of personal pledge is a personal liability of a disqualified person.

This can become confusing. While I cannot legally pledge the foundation's money to my child's school, I *can* go to the foundation, tell the board about the new science building, and suggest a grant of $10,000 toward this worthwhile project. If the board agrees, this type of grant is legal and appropriate.

The difference between these two scenarios is nuanced. While I can tell my child's school, "I would like my foundation to donate money. Let me run it by them," I cannot actually *promise* the money on behalf of the foundation.

When it comes to pledges, it's not the gift or where it's going that causes an issue. It's *how* the gift is extended. Foundation funding must be disbursed as grants rather than promised personal pledges, even if the allocation of the money looks identical.

Scholarship Beneficiaries

Many foundations fund scholarships—and they are perfectly within their right to do so. However, it is generally not appropriate for foundations to determine which students receive those scholarships.

Based on the regulations around self-dealing (as well as common sense), it's fairly obvious that no one related to a foundation board member can benefit from foundation scholarships. However, a common scenario is that a foundation donates money to a school, and the school then determines who the scholarship recipient will be. Someone on the foundation board then hears of a tertiary party who could use those funds and contacts the school to suggest the scholarship be given to that individual.

This is also illegal.

It is a best practice to refrain from any part in the process of determining scholarship recipients, even in cases in which potential recipients have no connection to the foundation. Foundations should have no role in influencing who receives scholarship funding.

In an ideal scenario, foundations will gift money to be put toward scholarships to a school. The school will then decide how to deploy those funds, without any specific input from the foundation.

This situation becomes more complicated in instances in which a foundation runs their own scholarship program. While it is within the scope of regulatory guidelines to do so, foundations must make a concerted effort to ensure that the allocation of these scholarships is handled in a way that is objective and completely transparent. In such an instance, it is highly advisable that the foundation brings in an expert to ensure that their scholarship program is being run according to the letter of the law. Big problems can result when there is even a suspicion that foundations might be influencing scholarship recipients.

An Alternative Option: Donor-Advised Funds

If you've read this far and feel like a family foundation is simply too complex for your taste, you may want to consider opening a donor-advised fund.

Donor-advised funds function just like a family foundation but involve no more than depositing your gift into what is essentially an investment account. Opening this account is a simple process that generally takes no more than a few days. Minimum contributions generally begin around $50,000.

As with foundations, once these funds are given to your donor-advised fund, they are irrevocable and become public property. You typically designate a local community foundation to serve as the custodian of these funds and do the work of overseeing their administration. This includes administrative work, record keeping, tax reporting, and grant administration. The community foundations generally charge a nominal fee of between 0.5 and 1 percent per year to keep the account in compliance with regulations.

While the community foundation assumes responsibility for the funds and their allocation, you will act as an advisor. You will make recommendations about how to grant the funds you contributed and over what amount of time. Though the charitable sponsor has the authority to approve or deny those recommendations, this rarely occurs unless the beneficiary organization is somehow disqualified.

The community foundation may provide a basic framework for the investment of funds, much like you would receive from an institution such as Schwab or Fidelity. Beyond that, a community foundation will generally not provide investment advice. They do add real value by providing a stable of philanthropic advisors to assist in the grant-making process.

In the case of a donor-advised fund, you can still work with a CIO if you have allocated a significant amount of money to your fund (usually $5 million or more). In this case, a CIO could be engaged to help with the asset allocation and investment selection process much like they would for a family foundation.

There are also several tax benefits to this strategy. You receive an income tax deduction from the moment the funds are designated to the account, regardless of the period of time over which they are distributed.

You will incur no capital gains tax on gifts of appreciated assets, nor will your funds be subject to estate taxes. Your investments can appreciate tax-free. If you are subject to an alternative minimum tax (AMT), your contribution will reduce your AMT impact.

Unlike a family foundation, there is no separate tax return, which means you enjoy greater privacy. You do not have the same level of fiduciary responsibility. The need for board meetings and other administrative and managerial tasks is also done away with. Finally, if you are not satisfied with your DAF partner, you can generally transfer your fund to another community foundation with little effort.

Donor-advised funds are becoming increasingly popular because they're nimble, and easy to establish and manage. According to the National Philanthropic Trust, in 2017, there were 463,622 individual donor-advised funds across the country. Donors contributed $29.23 billion to these donor-advised funds and used them to recommend $19.08 billion in grants to qualified charities. Both grants and contributions reached record highs. Charitable assets in donor-advised funds totaled $110.01 billion, surpassing the $100 billion mark for the first time.

They also tend to be particularly attractive to people in the tech industry, because—like tech—donor-advised funds are quick and efficient. For example, according to *The New York Times*, in December 2012, just months after Facebook went public, Mr. Zuckerberg donated $500 million of Facebook shares to a donor-advised fund at the Silicon Valley Community Foundation.[2]

---

2 David Gelles, "How Tech Billionaires Hack Their Taxes With A Philanthropic Loophole," *The New York Times*, August 3, 2018, *https://www.nytimes.com/2018/08/03/business/donor-advised-funds-tech-tax.html*

In a Nutshell

Perhaps you've noticed that the common denominator among all five of these common mistakes is that, rather than any of these activities being outright illegal, they all involve crossing an often blurry line. In cases where a foundation is not fully versed in the specifics of the applicable laws and regulations, it's all too easy to cross into a gray area without even being aware of it.

In addition to your foundation's own stable of trusted resources, the Council on Foundations (www.cof.org) is an excellent resource for further information on the regulations associated with these common mistakes and any other gray areas you might encounter. This nonprofit organization was established with the express purpose of serving family and community foundations.

CONCLUSION

THIS BUSINESS IS PERSONAL

Go confidently in the direction of your dreams.
Live the life you have imagined.
—Henry David Thoreau

It's an amazing time for foundations. They've never played a bigger role in our society than they do today, and their assets have never been as large as they are right now. Collectively, we are becoming more engaged in philanthropy.

At the same time, the changing regulatory environment, the volatility of the financial markets, and complexity of investment strategies requires a more professional approach than ever before. The regulatory requirements are now more difficult to adhere to. Due to the level of transparency now required of foundations, never before have foundations had to contend with the level of public visibility and awareness than they do today.

Let's Have Coffee

If you are involved in your family foundation and feel overwhelmed, know you do not have to traverse this complicated landscape alone. The first step is to have coffee with me.

I created *www.HaveCoffeeWithBruce.com* because I truly believe that the first step in any professional relationship is the relationship itself. You can't hire someone on blind faith and then get to know them later with any sort of guarantee that you will feel good about the ultimate outcome of your partnership. This is particularly true when it comes to managing your foundation's assets. There is so much at stake on so many levels.

I created **www.HaveCoffeeWithBruce.com** because I truly believe that the first step in any professional relationship is the relationship itself.

Over a cup of coffee, you'll get to know me and learn about Relevant Wealth's history working with foundations. Most importantly, you'll discover my personal passion for working with philanthropists. This social visit also gives me a chance to get to know you and your foundation, and to hear what's important to you.

This first meeting together is partly informal and partly formal. We'll talk about your foundation's history of giving, investment strategies, and past relationships. I'll tell you about our services and how we engage with our foundations.

Then, based on our conversation, we'll determine whether or not to further discuss your partnership with Relevant Wealth Advisors to manage your foundation's investments. If it appears that we can bring additional value to your foundation's operations and increase your philanthropic mission through our thorough and mindful investment management, we will then provide a complimentary and confidential "stress test" of your investment process.

During our stress test, we'll ask a series of specific questions to establish your foundation's mission and purpose. After providing a list of specific documents we need to review, we get to work analyzing your information. This valuable experience will identify any gaps you may not realize exist in your current operations and investment strategies, giving you the information you need to know if a CIO would be a good addition to your foundation.

If we believe we can add real value and promote positive growth, we develop a plan and lay out how we would work together to bring your foundation to a higher level of performance, not just in terms of your investment strategy, but also with reporting, documentation, and board engagement.

Through this review process, we will strive to build the level of trust a foundation and CIO need to truly benefit from a partnership. For long-term relationships to be successful, there have to be long-term benefits. That's easily promised but rarely delivered.

It all begins with that first cup of coffee, where we get to know one another and see if a high level of compatibility exists. Unlike hiring professionals to perform accounting, bookkeeping, or legal work, managing a foundation's investments is far more personal. This kind of partnership requires more engagement. If you don't have the personal connection so important in relationships that demand a great deal of trust, you're not going to find the success you want.

I invite you to take that important first step and have coffee with Bruce!

ACKNOWLEDGMENTS

First, I want to acknowledge my wife, Sara. Not sure where I'd be without you, and I'm grateful for your support and the journey we're on. Thank you for being my partner in life. I love you.

Second, I want to thank my amazing Relevant Wealth team. As we often say at RWA, if you want to go fast, go alone; if you want to go far, go together. My loyal team brings real expertise to our clients and has made it possible for me to grow and elevate our company.

Third, I have unending gratitude for my clients, many of whom I have known for decades. We've successfully navigated several economic cycles together, including the Great Recession. Their confidence in my advice and willingness to focus on what really matters has allowed all of us to live the lives of our dreams.

Finally, I want to thank the amazing Scribe team who helped me fulfill my vision of writing a book about one of my greatest passions. A special thank you to Meghan McCracken and Ellie Cole. Their focused expertise, positive energy, and unending patience were instrumental in helping me navigate the entire process. I will always be grateful for their contribution.

ABOUT THE AUTHOR

Bruce Raabe is the founder of Relevant Wealth Advisors and regularly leverages over twenty years of professional experience to develop technology-based strategic investment initiatives for high-net-worth families and private foundations. His expertise in investment policy development, asset allocation, and foundation regulatory requirements has allowed him to develop an understanding of the special circumstances surrounding the financial needs and goals of his private foundation clients.

Bruce is a licensed private pilot and enjoys outdoor activities with his wife, Sara, and three children. He holds several professional designations and regularly volunteers on numerous nonprofit boards in the San Francisco Bay Area.